PARENTING ADULT CHILDREN

Parenting Adult Children

A Practical Guide to Navigating
Your Evolving Relationship

Kate McNulty, LCSW

ROCKRIDGE
PRESS

For general information on our other products and services or to obtain technical support, please contact our Customer Care Department within the United States at (866) 744-2665, or outside the United States at (510) 253-0500.

Rockridge Press publishes its books in a variety of electronic and print formats. Some content that appears in print may not be available in electronic books, and vice versa.

TRADEMARKS: Rockridge Press and the Rockridge Press logo are trademarks or registered trademarks of Callisto Media Inc. and/or its affiliates, in the United States and other countries, and may not be used without written permission. All other trademarks are the property of their respective owners. Rockridge Press is not associated with any product or vendor mentioned in this book.

Interior and Cover Designer: Brian Lewis
Art Producer: Samantha Ulban
Editor: Carolyn Abate
Production Manager: Michael Kay
Production Editor: Melissa Edeburn

All images used under license © Shutterstock.com.
Author photo courtesy of Brian McDonnell.

ISBN: Print 978-1-64876-943-6 | eBook 978-1-64876-944-3

R0

To my parents, who came from meager beginnings to build lives of learning and imagination that continue to inspire.

Contents

Introduction: Parents, Take Heart

Parenting doesn't necessarily get easier when your children are grown. But it does change.

If you're facing challenges navigating your relationship with your grown-up kid, take heart. Think of the lifetime of observation and experiences you have accumulated as a parent. I bet you still remember the early stages of getting used to life with your child. Most parents can admit to at least a fleeting moment of wondering how they'd ever be able to deal with total responsibility for—gulp—someone else's life.

In those early days, new moms and dads can't comprehend what that responsibility will involve. Just as children grow into adults, we have to grow into parents. Our minds have not built a sufficient catalog of experiences to grasp how much we will change, be challenged, suffer, and struggle right along with our children. But now you have all those experiences on which to draw as your relationship with your child evolves into something new.

Not that raising kids is all bad. Children transport us to states of exuberant joy, giddiness, and hilarity that are hard to achieve as adults. Okay, some of that may be sleep deprivation.

I appreciate what you're going through as a parent struggling to reconnect with your adult child. My clinical experience has brought me in contact with many families facing this issue, and I'll rely on that experience to help you articulate and make progress on your family relationship goals. I'll also draw on my experience of being someone's adult child and of raising two children who are, so far at least, happy and flourishing well into their 20s.

Each family history is singular. Even so, in this book you'll find a variety of stories that cover a range of ages—from parents who are helping their children move out for the first time to grandparents who are navigating different parenting philosophies. Though you can see that your child has reached full adulthood, adjusting to their changes can be challenging. I invite you to consider how the anecdotes and themes behind these stories hold meaning for you and can spark some new insights.

The goal of *Parenting Adult Children* is to help you reconnect with your adult child by empowering you with the communication and boundary-setting skills you need and offering context for common areas of conflict so that you can understand what's underlying the clash. To accomplish this goal, we've organized the chapters into three parts:

Part 1 presents an overview of the changes families may experience as a young adult progresses through predictable stages to full adulthood. You'll find questions that encourage you to reflect on your expectations and values. And you'll learn about communication tools to help you improve your relationship with your adult child.

Part 2 demonstrates how those tools work by presenting common scenarios and conflict areas between parents and adult children and by discussing the strategies that bring a peaceful resolution.

Part 3 covers a variety of potential challenges that involve you, your adult child, and other people—partners, in-laws, grandchildren, and other family members.

The conclusion reviews your goals and the lessons learned throughout the book and offers encouragement and support in your journey toward a deeper connection with your adult child.

PART ONE

Your Evolving Relationship with Your Adult Child

It's easy to love a baby. We're biologically wired to adore big expressive eyes, oversized heads, and roly-poly bodies. Why else would Disney's cutest and cuddliest characters share these traits?

That instinctive love is deepened as children develop into individuals, and we get to know their personalities and temperaments. And as our children grow and their needs change, our involvement as parents changes. Many can find it surprising, though, that their parental status doesn't neatly wrap up on their child's 18th birthday—or even their 21st. Rather, the parental role just continues to change.

Chapter 1

A Changing Relationship

To establish a stronger relationship with your child, start by examining where that relationship stands today. Though the two of you will always be parent and child, your dynamic should move with time toward that of peer-to-peer between independent adults. If that bond isn't working smoothly, consider this situation an opportunity to examine the expectations you have as a parent, to reflect on your values, and to decide on the goals you have for reconnecting with your child. With that mindset, begin exploring concepts and exercises related to healthy communication skills and habits you can adopt in order to achieve the connection with your child you truly want.

Strong Foundation

In my work as a family therapist, I've found that people typically value family closeness more than any professional accomplishments or public recognition, which is why conflict in a family can feel so overwhelming. Disagreements are a part of life. People who love each other don't always see eye to eye. But if every argument or slight feels like it might do irreparable damage to a relationship you treasure, the tension can feel unbearable.

With a strong foundation of healthy communication habits—active listening, communicating respectfully, managing and de-escalating conflict, and other techniques you'll learn in these pages—your relationship with your adult child can weather almost anything.

A New Understanding

The strong foundation you're building starts with understanding that the parent-child relationship continues to evolve throughout life. Your relationship with your toddler was different than your relationship with your teenager. Helping an adult child achieve sufficient autonomy is a universal experience for families and includes a shift to an adult-to-adult rapport between you and the child you've guided into adulthood. You're still a parent, but just as the requirements of parenting changed when your child learned to walk, started school, got a driver's license, and started dating, so they will change when your child reaches adulthood.

A New Phase of Parenting

You were a caregiver and a confidant for your child earlier in life. Bathing your little one, reading bedtime stories, and singing in the car on the way to visit the grandparents are fond memories now. Even though your adult relationship with your grown child brings you new and rewarding experiences, mourning the loss of your earlier role is perfectly normal. Indulge nostalgic feelings by reminiscing about them and doing activities such as scrapbooking, making photo albums, or converting old home movies to digital format.

Learning to Let Go

Some parents have an easier time than others letting go of control as adult children begin to carve out their own lives. If you're finding it difficult to let your child take the wheel, think back to your own early adulthood. Remember how much you learned as a young person by enduring difficult times and coming out on the other side? Whereas stepping in and trying to solve your adult child's problems may be tempting, refraining from parental interference is likely to preserve your relationship. If you spend more time listening to your child explain their situation than talking about what they should do, there is little cause for argument. And the next time they need a sounding board, your child will turn to you.

It's a Brave New World

The pressures and challenges your adult child faces are not the same as those you faced. Due to forces beyond their control, young adults today are delayed in achieving adult milestones. As one example, a 2020 report by the Pew Research Center confirms that over half of adults ages 18 to 29 live with their parents. And with good reason. Since 2001, renters' income has not matched the rise in rental costs.

Low-income renters often must pay more than half their salary in rent, well above the standard recommendation of budgeting one-third of income for housing. Due to these economic trends, young people defer marriage and parenthood until later in life. Living together before marriage has become socially acceptable. The average age of a bride is now 27, compared to 20 in 1960. The groom who would have been 22 in 1960 is now 29, a significant difference in maturity.

It's a Partnership

When your child knows they have your encouragement, they can feel like they have the wind at their back. Here are five ways to be a partner to your adult child:

Let your child learn from their errors without criticizing or backseat driving. They own their life.

Listen for something you can agree with and remark only on that.

If they ask for a loan but you've had issues with trust, settle on a token amount, or let them borrow something that will help their situation.

Ask their opinions on issues of the day, dilemmas you're facing, or current stories highlighted in the media.

Honor confidences. Keep to any agreement of privacy for personal information.

Reflect on the Relationship You Want

You're probably reading this book because something in your relationship with your child isn't working. But equally as important as identifying the problems is having a clear sense of what a healthy, functioning, rewarding connection with your adult child would mean to you. What kind of relationship do you want?

Consider your goals for your relationship with your adult child. Talk about your parent-child relationship with your partner, a friend, or a family member. Meeting with a support group, religious leader, or therapist can make a difference. We all gain from someone else's perspective.

Your Goals. As you reflect on the questions and exercises in this book, you may find writing down your goals in a journal or notebook to be helpful so you can refer back to your responses as you work your way through the examples in part 2. Here are some of the goals I hear most often from the families I work with in my practice:

Strengthening or Renewing Ties. You may want to reconnect with a child who you've fallen out of touch with or reaffirm your connection with a child as they set out on their own.

Setting Boundaries. Now that you're both adults, you may be wondering how involved you will be in each other's lives. You may wish to set ground rules for an adult who's had to move back home.

Encouraging Independence. You may wish to know how to help your child leave the nest while supporting their effort to fly.

Improving "Street Smarts." You may want your child to be prepared for what they may encounter in what can be a scary world.

Overcoming Setbacks. You may want to assist a child burdened by obstacles, circumstances, or special needs that require extra effort or resources to handle.

Whatever situations are keeping you from your goals, you most definitely are not alone. No family is perfect, however much they may seem so on the surface. In this book, you'll read about families who faced conflicts of all sorts, and their stories will show what you can do to pivot to a positive direction.

Your Values. We all inherit values from the family we grew up with. You have specific values you hold dear as an individual; you also share values with your spouse and with your community or cultural group. And the values that hold meaning for you will be the ones that you transmit to the next generation.

Those values are transmitted to your children, knowingly or not; people learn from their parents' behavior more than what they say. Values are still an important part of the conversations you have with your children, even though they are grown. How have your values changed as you have matured while raising your family?

Their Goals. You and your young adult are probably already discussing the priorities in their lives. Knowing them as you do, what can you guess about their point of view and wishes for themselves? This imaginative exercise is essential if your family is experiencing conflict or if your child has become distant from you. Your child's actions or refusals have some reason behind them, and often that reason is tied to their goals in life. Empathizing and trying to sort out your child's side of the equation will unearth clues about behaviors that seem stuck or frustrating to you.

Their Values. Your young adult is still forming their character and belief system. They may already have passionate ideas about moral issues or identify with a life philosophy. Think back to your younger self. Do you recall the intensity of your beliefs, how passionately you held on to your ideals?

Instead of debating convictions, consider your child's values. Thinking back on their childhood, ask yourself what seemed to interest or engage them. What were they like when they were excited about something?

Understanding them is crucial for resolving conflict and communicating with respect.

Avoid Drifting Apart

If you have a grown child with a private temperament, the balancing act of when to approach them and when to give them space can be a delicate one. Here are some methods for maintaining a tendril of connection:

Feed them generously. Young adults are usually hungry and low on money! Cook them meals or venture to a new restaurant together.

Keep conversations light. Detour around stressful topics and be ready with anecdotes or "dad" jokes.

Respect boundaries. If they don't want to talk about something, move on or ask, "When would be a better time to catch up about this?"

Reflection Questions

» When talking with your child, do you invite pleasant conversation as well as more serious discussion? Try offering observations about, say, current events or life in your area, rather than focusing only or mainly on the young adult's anticipated hire or move-out date.

» Do you indicate respect for your adult child's time? Even if you know they're not busy, ask if it's a good time to check in when you initiate a conversation. Model the behavior you want to receive.

» Are you demonstrating openness in your communication? You can help avoid your adult child shutting down during a chat by paying attention to your posture and voice. We'll cover more about this topic in the next chapter.

Chapter 2

Building Your Communication Foundation

Now that you better understand how a parent's role changes throughout life, it's time to equip yourself with the tools to stay connected—or to reconnect—with your adult child. This chapter introduces methods parents can use to build a strong foundation of healthy communication habits. There are no right answers for challenges that arise between you and your adult child because the solutions depend on your respective values and personalities. But some of the principles of human behavior we'll cover here may help you resolve your particular issues.

Healthy Communication

As we noted in chapter 1 (see page 4), family closeness is impossible without healthy communication. That sounds straightforward enough—we all want to be heard, just as we all want to hear and understand the people close to us—but healthy communication is not always easy to achieve. As every younger generation keeps growing and changing, so does the way their parents communicate with them. Despite your best intentions, you may find it hard to break old habits and update your communication style to meet your child's current needs. This difficulty can lead to a communication breakdown that can spark conflict.

Let's look at the principles of healthy communication and some methods you can use to put them into action.

Active Listening

Have you ever been talking to someone, only to find yourself wondering if they heard a single thing you were saying? It can be hard to tell if a listener is actually listening to you rather than daydreaming or just ignoring your voice. That's where *active listening* comes in. During active listening, the one doing the listening signals to the speaker in various ways that they are participating in the conversation. Here are three methods of active listening to try:

Engage in emotional reflection. In this method, the listener offers a response that indicates understanding and that affirms the perspective of the speaker. For example, if Maya says to her dad, Cruz, that she's discouraged by the high costs of rent where she wants to live, he might reply, "I know you've been looking hard. Sounds like there's not much in your price range." Cruz is serving as a mirror for his daughter's feelings, showing he understands she's tiring of her housing search.

This mirroring provides Maya with the sense that she's not alone in her difficult task.

Ask open-ended questions. The listener in this method offers questions about what the speaker is saying to demonstrate interest. In the emotional reflection example, Cruz can ask questions that invite Maya to share more information: "What do you like about that neighborhood?" or "Is there anything you need from me? Our budget is still tight, but maybe I can help you somehow. Let me know if you think of anything, okay?" Although Cruz cannot solve her problem, his form of emotional support shows that he, as the parent, is right alongside Maya as she strives for her goals.

Summarize what you've heard. This method involves the listener repeating in their own words what the speaker has said in order to show that the listener understands. Doing so helps both the listener and speaker identify priorities. If Cruz were to say, "It sounds like the things that matter most to you are staying within your budget and having transportation nearby," he'd demonstrate that he's paying close attention, is involved with Maya, and is thinking about her dilemma.

Communicate with Respect

Roles shift as parents accompany young adults toward maturity, and the best way to show your grown child how you want them to treat you is to extend the respect you expect in return. Demonstrating respect in any adult relationship is always a worthy investment. Prioritizing respectful behavior may feel a bit different from the more authoritarian approach you're used to, but the change reflects the new and rewarding relationship of two adults interacting on a peer level. Here are some ways to engage in this type of communication:

Have conversations instead of lecturing. When speaking to your adult child, use good manners and be polite, just as you taught them to do when they were young. Address your child as you would a friend or neighbor. Avoid giving unsolicited opinions and ask permission to raise your concerns when a conflict arises. Remember that you can still be a guiding influence without holding your authority over your child. Be an advisor instead of a criticizer.

Ask questions and invite discussion. Take your adult child seriously and demonstrate your interest in having a peer relationship; seek their perspective and listen when they offer it. Even superficial subjects such as sports or popular media open up conversations that feel approachable. This approach paves the way to talking about more controversial topics later when you have built back rapport.

Pay attention to tone and body language. It's easy to send a nonverbal disrespectful message without realizing it. Turn your body toward your child when talking to them, showing that they have your full attention. Maintain a relaxed posture and avoid obstacles such as crossed arms or holding objects in front of you. Leave your phone alone, even if your child is looking at theirs (another example of modeling the behavior you want to receive).

Notice any tension in your body when you speak. How does a clenched posture affect the sound of your voice? Take your time when speaking; brief pauses in the conversation will allow you to breathe freely.

Assume competence. As a parent, you may never lose the instinct to help your child. But you can offer resources or share information while supporting your child as a capable person who can make their own decisions. Acknowledge any efforts your child is making, even if the way they are going about something is not how you would do it. If your young adult is absorbed in terrible music, games that seem silly, or a cause you don't particularly care about, you can still stretch yourself to try and engage with their interests. To be part of their world, you must respect and validate what is important to them.

Affirm and Encourage

Because your adult child is pulling away to establish their own life, it will be up to you to keep your connection alive. If your child hears encouragement and admiration toward them from you, your words can act as a force of gravity that keeps you in each other's orbits. Thanking your child for sharing the name of a restaurant they discovered or a movie they recommended shows them you are moving the relationship toward that of peer adults. The following are ways to connect with your adult child through positive, encouraging behavior.

Suggest and affirm. Rather than telling your adult child what to do, try showing them how to walk through a problem. Ask them questions about their reasoning and conclusions to show you are standing alongside them, shoulder to shoulder. Validating a problem as complicated or painful is also helpful. Supportive parents admit their own past misjudgments, tell stories of their foibles, and affirm that life is mostly a series of experiments that may or may not turn out as expected.

Ask before giving advice. This method can be a tough. You may not be accustomed to asking permission from your children, but now that they're grown, it's time to acknowledge your changing relationship. Instead of just offering your advice, ask, "Is this a good time to talk?" or "Would you be interested in some of my thoughts?" Questions like these probably seem formal or unnecessary, but posing them is a small effort to ensure that your child is motivated to spend time with you. And acknowledging their adult status makes a difference, even if they don't always act like adults. Just as you don't reach out and wipe food off their face or tell them what to wear anymore, you don't want to be the only one to set the terms for conversation. Instead, show respect by letting them decide what advice they want to hear from you.

Refrain from saying "I told you so." Creating the new phase of your relationship requires you to allow your child to make some of their own salvageable mistakes. Let go of the need to show off your knowledge or prove that you knew better.

Conflict Management

When dealing with the people you've known their whole lives, and most of yours, feelings sometimes run hot. But it's possible to constructively express emotions, even when they're intense. In the past, therapists would encourage families to eliminate conflict as much as possible, but decades of psychological research have shown the valuable learning opportunities in struggle. Handling conflict effectively—that is, conflict management—actually leads to increased family closeness. Let's take a closer look at this concept.

De-escalate a Conflict

Successful conflict management brings fewer worries and headaches and encourages a situation in which the parents are more likely to enjoy the young adults in their lives. Here are some suggestions to help you keep your cool when conflict arises:

Refrain from blaming. A common reaction to negative emotions is blame because reflecting and taking responsibility require effort we can't always expend in the moment. Concluding that someone else caused the problem or distress we are experiencing is easier and brings us temporary relief. Being the target of blame is a problem, though, because receiving blame creates an emotional reaction that interferes with the brain's ability to listen and learn. In any conflict it's preferable to stop, think, and reason your way through how to handle things.

Manage defensiveness. Like blame, defensiveness is another near-automatic response to conflict. We want to be respected so we try to protect ourselves by justifying why we are right and others are wrong. When you decide the priority is to preserve your relationships above all else, you are less likely to find fault. What's the value of denying a mistake or hiding negative emotions when what you really want is a close lifelong relationship with your offspring?

Take a break. When the situation gets emotionally demanding, take a break before doing significant damage to the relationship. None of us are at our best when we are distressed; we're not capable of thinking clearly or choosing our words carefully in a state of high emotion. Instead, do damage control by saying, "Let's talk later," or "I'm going to have to think about this," and walking away. Come back when you have your composure again.

Make repairs. With every remark, each person in an argument has the power to make the situation better or worse. As the parent, you are better equipped than your adult child to steer the conversation in a positive direction. Repairing someone's wounded pride or hurt feelings through kindness, apologies, or expressions of love and affection can heal a relationship and show your good intentions.

Employ the 5:1 ratio. During arguments, family members with good relationships manage to include pleasant or understanding comments along with harsh or critical words. Positive statements in a conversation are like deposits to the fund of good feelings in your relationship, whereas each negative remark is like making a withdrawal. Be sure your ratio of positive to negative remarks favors the positive. Research suggests that making five encouraging, supportive statements for every negative one is the best practice.

Setting Boundaries

Personal boundaries are the limitations we ask for in our relationships. Your boundaries are yours to set—based on your physical, financial, or emotional needs. Letting people know your availability and limitations can become complicated when guilt, a wish to please others, or a desire to avoid conflict is present. In the long run, however, you make life more comfortable for yourself and others when you let people know what to expect.

The Benefits of Boundaries (for You and Them)

In the absence of proper boundaries set by your adult child, you may believe it's okay and within your right to impose your will on their lives. When they do have boundaries, your adult child can develop and maintain independence from you, their parents. Here are some of the benefits:

Healthy modeling. We've all experienced the difference between someone *telling* us how to do something from someone *showing* us how to do it. People usually learn faster and remember better when someone shows them. Remember, your grown child is still learning from you, and they will continue to do so throughout their life. It's instructive for them to see you put yourself first, even if it means you decline a request they made or they have to delay an activity they want to do. Your child will see you taking care of yourself. They, too, need to learn how to manage their time and energy capably.

Conserving your resources. Most people have busy lives and feel short on time. One everyday use of boundaries is to get in the habit of saying no more often. Doing so helps you avoid getting overextended or feeling like you're in over your head. Remember that you are a resource for others, like the people in your family. You're a renewable resource in the sense that you need to replenish yourself with, say, food and rest. But that replenishment takes time and effort. Setting boundaries means you don't get all used up before you can renew.

Preventing resentment. Paying attention to your boundaries means leaving something for yourself. People who give too much of themselves (such as their time, belongings, space, or money) eventually feel they're being taken advantage of and that things are unfair. This tendency shifts thinking toward resentment and bitterness over time. As the parent, you have a responsibility to maintain sufficient boundaries so that you are able to maintain an ongoing, enduring connection with your child. Pace how much of the giving you are doing. As your child matures, expect increasing reciprocity, and you will not need to do as much to manage boundaries.

Define Your Boundaries

Setting boundaries is often a messy series of steps. Typically, we must go through trial and error to figure out what we can and can't handle in our relations with others. But it's worth the effort. Here are some steps to follow in setting your boundaries:

Make specific plans. When it comes to life with your young adult child, consider what you can *realistically* offer them and not just what you wish you could offer them. For example, if their car breaks down, can they borrow yours? On what days and for how long? How much advance notice would you want if the plan were to change?

Set clear expectations. Strive to say what you mean, or prepare to feel resentment or regret. Not up for loaning the car at all? Take the plunge and say so: "Thank you for letting me think this over. I know you need to get places, but I don't feel comfortable with you using the car. Here's what I could do: I could pay for a bus pass and budget X dollars to pay for rides this month, or I could put a set amount toward a used car." It's never too late to improve your communication style by speaking honestly about how you can and can't help. Your child will observe and take note of any efforts you make.

Affirm good judgment. Here's an important principle of teaching young children: "Catch them doing something right." Adults should offer praise when a child remembers to wash their hands before a meal or hang up their jacket without being prompted. This concept works for people of all ages. When you hear your young adult mention they put gas in the car before returning it or made sure a friend got home safely, take the opportunity to validate their maturity or thoughtfulness. Doing so is like watering a little sprout emerging from the earth; even if your child doesn't outwardly acknowledge what you've said, they'll soak up your recognition and approval, which will help them grow.

Reach Out

Whether you've had a recent conflict or you're just wondering what your child is up to these days, reach out to them. If they seem to forget you exist, don't take that to mean they don't care. Go ahead and take the first steps to initiate conversation. Remember, they're busy starting a whole new life (or should be), so keeping the connection alive may be up to you as they pursue new opportunities and experiences. There's no need to force deep, heart-to-heart talks upon your busy young adult. Small, light touches are useful for letting them know they are supported and loved, such as:

Send a thoughtful card. Now more than ever, the surprise of finding a personally addressed note in the mail is always fun. Especially when there's no occasion except your desire to say "Cheers" or "Hang in there."

Offer an invitation. Dinner is great, but less formal events can fit better into a busy schedule. How about a drink with snacks on the porch? Even a text message about current events or a funny situation you experienced is an opportunity to spark conversation.

Ask for help. A side-by-side shared activity is a good opportunity to chat. Ask for an afternoon of yard work help or a paint touch-up around the house.

Share small gifts. Offer your spare gift cards from store returns. Buy a family-size fancy cheese or chocolate assortment and split it up to share.

Make a field trip. Meet your busy young person on neutral turf, perhaps somewhere easy for them to get to. Visit a museum exhibit or sporting goods store or take whatever outing might interest both of you.

Caring for Yourself

With your children grown, you're now officially free to live as a restless spirit on the hot winds, so why not make the most of this new stage of your life? Self-care can be an opportunity to rediscover who you are apart from your role as a parent and caregiver. Giving yourself an enriching, satisfying life also helps you renew your energy levels so you can provide support and encouragement when your adult child needs it.

Seek out friends for impromptu events; make new friends if you're ready for more. You'll find many online and in-person parent groups to fit your situation. No matter what you're going through, somebody else is experiencing it, too.

If you're feeling lost or grieving, search online or ask your physician for a referral to a counselor or therapist, someone who has helped others with this new role.

Reflection Questions

» Are you letting your child make their own mistakes? Parents naturally want to shield their adult children from unnecessary expense or consequences. But the harsh reality is that because of the way the human brain works, most of us are experiential learners. We learn by doing, and lessons that result from our blunders and flops are the most vivid and lasting.

» What are some possible events or activities you could initiate for you and your adult child to enjoy together? Go beyond your own preferences and think of your child's tastes, interests, and personality. What subjects could they introduce to you? What topic would you like to explore that they could educate you about or support you in learning?

» What do you now realize you needed when you were your child's age? How is your adult child different from the way you were back then? How is your adult child similar to the way you were?

PART TWO

Common Conflicts with Your Adult Child

Each chapter in this section offers two scenarios related to a typical area of family conflict. We'll review stories that represent common dilemmas and see ways families can work through them. We'll also review the kinds of mistakes that can get made along the way. You'll learn how to handle similar situations in your own life—to deploy healthy communication strategies to connect with your adult child and maintain the peer-to-peer relationship that categorizes parenting at this stage of life.

Chapter 3

Failure to Launch

This chapter examines the family conflicts that can arise when a young adult has difficulty achieving independence and is struggling with milestones such as earning an income or managing their schedule and responsibilities. In extreme cases, this failure to launch into the next phase of their life could mean they rarely venture out of their room, much less leave the house.

Parents typically feel embarrassed and blame themselves in this situation. They hear about the achievements of the adult children of friends and family members and wonder what they did wrong. This emotional state contributes to isolation and reduces the number of people the family can reach out to for help. Both families in this chapter find resources to deal with these challenges in contrasting ways.

Stuck in a Time Warp

Slam!

Larry was startled by an abrupt crash followed by the house shaking while he watched the news. He realized that his 27-year-old son Justin was banging around upstairs again, likely yelling and throwing things because he screwed something up with his computer game.

Larry leaned over the edge of the couch and shouted toward the kitchen. "Angela! Can't you get him to hold it down? He's way too old to be acting this way!"

Larry's wife was already calling up the stairs. "Justin! That's enough! You're going to break something if you keep it up!" Justin yelled back, "I AM going to break something if you don't shut up!"

"Look, don't blame me," Angela told Larry as she joined him on the couch. "I tried to get him to come downstairs and eat dinner, but he's caught up in some quest or something. You know there's no stopping him when he gets in the middle of these things."

They could hear Justin continue to stomp around over their heads in his room. Larry and Angela wondered how they would ever get Justin to grow up. Their son worked at a (very) part-time retail job, and as far as they could tell, he had no new prospects. He'd only lasted a year at college, with lackluster performance. Angela and Larry offered him job leads and talked with him about going back to school, but it was hard to pull him away from the computer or stay with a conversation for long. When things got tense, Justin typically would go silent and retreat to his room.

It felt as though they were all trapped in time together with their son still living in his bedroom and depending on them for food and housing like an adolescent—and sometimes acting like one.

Scenario Analysis

Failure to launch, or FTL, has become such a common expression that it was even used as the title of a (poorly rated) movie. Using the term "failure" in the phrase is misleading because it suggests that achieving adult independence is a one-time event that either works or does not. Instead, a series of predictable steps is involved in a child transitioning to adulthood. Knowing the steps makes correcting an FTL situation more manageable.

Parent Viewpoint

Larry thought he probably hadn't been firm enough with his son, although he wasn't sure where he had gone wrong. He hated arguing and just wanted everybody in his family to be happy. Even though Larry didn't like the current situation with Justin, he still loved his son. He believed Justin was a good person who somehow had lost his way.

Angela knew Justin's presence at home was taking a toll on her marriage. She tried to support Larry in getting Justin to grow up and take some responsibility, but Justin was good at avoiding his parents. This situation couldn't go on forever. Justin was a grown man! By his age, she and Larry were already saving for a house and planning their wedding.

Adult Child Viewpoint

Justin didn't intend to stay with his parents forever. He had plans and was already starting to earn a little money online. Soon he would have enough to buy a new monitor and webcam. With new gear he could seriously monetize his Twitch stream and quit his job. His shifts were always getting cut anyway. Justin wanted to get his own place, but whenever he looked at the cost to rent an apartment, he got depressed and dropped the idea. He told himself not to stress over the details; it would all work out eventually. If his parents would just get off his case, his life would be in a lot better shape.

Strategy Breakdown

People outside the family typically imagine in this situation that parents are encouraging dependence or that their child is stubborn. Instead, it is usually a result of parents and the child lacking communication and problem-solving skills. Larry and Angela were going by instinct and didn't have the communication tools they needed to help their son. They tried to set boundaries, but as mentioned in chapter 2 (see page 20), boundary setting can be a trial-and-error process. Angela tended to get impatient around the issue of setting limits and would blow up at Justin. Larry would lecture him, telling him what he thought he should be doing instead of respectfully conversing with him as a peer. Neither parent knew how to capably manage conflict.

Angela and Larry decided to give Larry's sister Tina a call. She had three kids who had already moved away from home, and they all seemed to be doing well. They ended up having a series of conversations about how to help Justin. Following Tina's pointers, they employed the following strategies:

Engage in respectful communication. Larry and Angela started by leaving Justin a note, explaining they wanted to "talk over everybody's plans" the following weekend. In this way, they showed respect for his time, giving him a chance to prepare rather than suddenly demanding a conference.

Converse as equals. By emphasizing encouragement, they showed Justin they were on his side.

Ask open-ended questions. In the past, Larry had expressed his frustration via loaded questions like "So, are they giving you more hours?" which led to angry confrontations. This time, he followed Tina's suggested script and asked

Justin, "What are you thinking for your future, Justin? We want to know what kind of help you need."

Set boundaries. Larry moved the conversation forward by setting the expectation that he and Angela had decided on. "Your mom and I are thinking maybe you can stay another three months. What do you think about that?"

Justin looked uncomfortable but didn't lose his cool. "Yeah," he told them. "That's about what I was thinking, too. I have been looking around for a place. You know I'm trying to make money online, but I need some more equipment before I can do that."

"Well, that's good," Larry responded. "I'm glad you're thinking about how to make more money. If you need a jump start to get a deposit for a new place, we can talk about that. Angela added, "There's plenty of yard work around here. We can agree on what we'd owe you, if you're willing to handle that."

By conversing respectfully and communicating to him as supportive adults, his parents were able to steer him toward more realistic thinking. They made their expectations clear without lecturing or trying to demand that Justin step up and take more responsibility. Rather than complaining, they focused on what help they were willing to offer him.

Potential Pitfalls

Parents get some harsh advice about coping with FTL. But research doesn't support a tough love approach. Refrain from these tactics:

Punishing. If they're living with you, don't do things like removing their bedroom door or otherwise refusing to grant privacy. Belittling or humiliating someone who is already struggling makes matters worse.

Shaming. To respect your child's privacy, keep this problem within the family or consult a professional. Choose a trusted confidant to vent to if you must as long as they won't share the story.

Taking legal measures. Only in the most desperate circumstances is it advisable to call the law or use the courts to resolve a family dispute. Many other options are available before considering lockouts or eviction.

Tips to Remember

» **Try to be patient.** Inevitably, your adult child will leave someday. With FTL, your job is helping them do what they are already destined to do—grow up.

» **Examine your role.** In family systems, everyone contributes to the problem even if, as in Justin's case, his parents were merely allowing a situation to continue. Your best chance for making progress involves solving this riddle: What is your part? When you get perspective on what you do to keep the pattern going, you have identified where you have the power to make a change. Much like using a fulcrum to shift a load, you can change the family dynamic.

» **Consider another point of view.** We are sometimes too close to the problem to make sense of it. A friend or therapist can help you see your role.

Steps toward Reconnection

If issues relating to FTL have put distance between you and your child, don't let too much time pass before making repairs. Take initiative to mend any rift, even if you have legitimate grievances. The parent's responsibility is to be the bigger person.

Avoid holding a grudge. Better to either have your say about why you feel wronged or decide not to hold on to your anger.

Be willing to apologize. Express hurt feelings only if you must and try to move on. Practice humility.

Let bygones be bygones. If you and your adult child have drifted apart, explaining your side of an argument or justifying why you said what you said probably serves litle purpose. Keep your eye on the end goal of a satisfying relationship with your child.

If I Leave

Tyler was a 23-year-old with an active social life, both online and in his local community. He worked as a restaurant dishwasher and had always lived at home with his mother Danielle, a single parent. She worked as a server at a different restaurant, and her income varied based on season and economic fluctuations.

Much of Tyler's social life revolved around attending cosplay conventions, where participants wear elaborate handmade costumes in imitation of their favorite video game or movie characters. Travel expenses and material costs left Tyler living paycheck to paycheck without making any substantial financial contribution to the household.

As time went on, Danielle's work friends had urged her to get Tyler to either pay his way or move out. She enjoyed her son's company and delighted in his hobbies with him, but the two of them were often short on money. Also, Danielle had been getting to know one of the new cooks at work and realized she wanted the freedom to date and maybe occasionally bring an overnight guest home.

Danielle got vicarious enjoyment out of Tyler's crazy social life, and he could always make her laugh. She didn't want to make Tyler feel rejected, but Danielle suspected it was time for both of them to move on with their lives. One evening when the two of them were laughing over the photos on Tyler's phone, Danielle raised the topic: "Honey, do you ever think about getting your own place, where you could have your friends over?"

Tyler looked offended. "Are you saying I should get out?" he asked her. "What am I supposed to do? You know I could never afford my own place." He rolled his eyes. "Anyway, you're the one who always wants me to entertain you. You don't even have a life of your own. All you do is work."

Danielle felt stung but kept her composure. "You're right, Tyler," she told him. "I'm just starting to realize you're grown now. It's getting to be time for you to go out on your own. Let's sit down soon and talk about how to make it happen. We can figure things out. We always do."

Scenario Analysis

This conversation was unplanned; Tyler was startled when Danielle launched into the topic seemingly out of nowhere. He became defensive and lashed out at her. Although their talk had an awkward beginning, Danielle salvaged it skillfully. She believed in Tyler's creativity and talent. She knew if he got excited about the idea of living independently, he would take the idea and run with it.

Parent Viewpoint

Danielle jumped into a pivotal conversation unprepared. As she thought about it later, she recognized she hadn't been clear to him about her expectations—she hadn't even determined what they were. She realized she wasn't sure what was possible or realistic. She didn't know how much Tyler was earning—surely not much—or the costs of his cosplay lifestyle. Not having prepared for the discussion herself, she realized now the unfairness in expecting him to know anything about how to get an apartment. She felt hurt and defensive at his reaction but had to admit that her lack of tact had made for bad communication.

Adult Child Viewpoint

Tyler knew some people his age who lived on their own but didn't know how they could afford it. Most of his friends still lived with their folks. Adult life looked like one huge headache; he had no idea how to make enough money to get an apartment or pay bills. Plus, if he moved out, who would make his mother laugh or help her forget about her sore feet and cranky customers? Didn't his mother appreciate having him around? Where was this sudden pressure to move out coming from?

Strategy Breakdown

Parents can tell young people how to handle new responsibilities, but it's even more important to convey the notion that adult life consists of a set of skills that can be learned, such as reconciling a checking account or hanging curtains. You needed someone to show you, right? Parents can encourage young adults to admit what they don't know, seek resources, and ask as many questions as they need to.

After raising the topic led to trouble, Danielle realized that she'd need to outline expectations for Tyler while sharing her values of resourcefulness and flexibility. Here are the communication strategies Danielle used to ensure a better conversation the second time around:

Conflict management. Danielle decided to invite Tyler out for coffee. She thought it might be better for them to discuss the possibilities away from home. Doing so would make it easier to walk away from any bad feelings or stress generated by the discussion.

Favoring the positive. Knowing that Tyler might get defensive again, Danielle followed the 5:1 approach mentioned in chapter 2 (see page 19). She made several positive statements for each negative or critical point she made. She started the conversation by talking about Tyler's good qualities: He made friends with everybody, he had passions and interests, he was artistic. She told Tyler she had confidence in him.

Active listening. Several times in their conversation, Danielle asked open-ended questions. Realizing that his mother was hearing what he was saying, Tyler opened up and admitted that he was scared about growing up. He also asked Danielle, "What's going to happen to you if I leave?" She realized that he felt responsible for her, something she'd need to fix before Tyler could move ahead. She assured him that once they had a plan for him, she could handle her own life.

Conversing with respect. Speaking with him as an equal, Danielle admitted that she hadn't known what she was doing when she first left her parents' home either, but she figured it out. She listed things she had to learn when finding a place to live, like how to read a lease, set up utilities, and make a budget. She told Tyler they would start talking about this next stage of life so that he could prepare.

Affirmation and encouragement. "I know it's not all going to happen at once, I don't expect that," Danielle told him. "I want you to remember, you already know a lot about how to plan and make things happen. You've just been doing other stuff. You can learn this, and I will help you." Danielle emphasized Tyler's capabilities, and since she genuinely admired and enjoyed him, it was easy to be sincere.

Potential Pitfalls

Are you wondering how to activate the ejector seat for your grown child? These familiar proverbs indicate why you should avoid a sense of urgency:

Rome wasn't built in a day. Your situation is indeed difficult, but it took a while to get here. You'll need to be patient with your child and yourself.

Haste makes waste. You can expect your child to depart eventually. Rushing will not help matters. Better to set them up for success than have hasty plans fall apart, causing them to feel incapable.

Keep your eyes on the prize. Above all, the objective is to preserve the relationship. If you succeed at "launching" but then your child never wants to contact you, what have you really accomplished?

Tips to Remember

» **Try using multiple channels.** When communicating about important issues, keep your message consistent but consider repeating it through multiple formats. Your child may respond better to one kind of communication over another, so consider all of your options—from in-person conversations to email.

» **Follow their method.** Many young people rely almost exclusively on texting. Text your adult child if that method of communication works for them.

» **Give them options.** If you're not sure about the best way to share your thoughts, ask your adult child directly, just as you would ask a colleague in a business or work setting. "Here are some things I'd like us to talk over. How would you like me to follow up? Can I count on you getting something back to me after the weekend?"

Reflection Questions

» What strengths and aptitudes do you see in your child? Are there any passions or fascinations you remember them displaying from a young age?

» How would you like to help your child envision or dream about their future?

» Does your child seem most comfortable with speaking, writing, or imagery? If you don't know, how could you raise this question with them?

» Do you enjoy relating anecdotes from your young adulthood? Do you have stories or dreams that feel too personal to share? What causes you to keep those to yourself?

Chapter 4

Financial Stability

If it seems to you that young adults of today take longer to grow up than in previous generations, you're correct—at least in terms of the events we associate with adulthood. Over the past 20 years, economic and cultural changes have pushed milestones such as marriage, buying a house, and parenthood to later in life. These things used to indicate that adults were on the path to maturing, yet, today, few young people are financially stable enough to afford child-rearing or their own home. Instead, parents must look to their child's emotional maturity, rather than their career path or financial stability, to track their progress toward adulthood. This chapter explores how parents grapple with their adult child's requests for temporary and ongoing assistance through the transition to full adulthood.

A Place of Her Own

Shanice showed up for dinner on time, greeting her mom, Vanessa, with a bouquet of flowers and giving her dad, Reggie, a peck on the cheek. As they sat together at the table, Shanice explained her situation. "Look," she said, "I know I've never had my own place, but my roommates party too much. I need quiet so I can concentrate when I study. I have a new place lined up. The only problem is, since my income isn't full-time yet, I need to ask you two to cosign for me."

Reggie responded, "I'm glad you want to focus on school. But you know, you're asking us to take on a big responsibility here. Tell me about your budget."

Shanice, knowing her dad, had prepared for this question. She got out her tablet and outlined her expenses and income from her work-study job. She acknowledged she would have to find an additional source of income to make her rent. "I'll find online work I can do from home," she said.

Reggie and Vanessa told their daughter they needed to think it over. As Shanice gathered her things to leave, Reggie hugged her tight and said, "Just keep working hard, Shanice. You're making us proud."

Scenario Analysis

Shanice was trying to make the most of her education and was behaving more maturely than her peers. Her forethought in preparing a budget to share with her parents impressed them. They knew she was asking for a helping hand, not an indulgence.

Nevertheless, the risk to Reggie and Vanessa if they cosigned was substantial. Their own credit status was only starting to improve as they paid down debt. And their budget was tight. They'd be risking a significant financial hit, with Shanice not sure how she was going to make her future rent obligations.

Parent Viewpoint

After Shanice left, Vanessa turned to Reggie and sighed. "I wish so much we could do this for her," she said.

Reggie kneaded his hands. "I know, but her plan's not realistic. And I don't want her to get spread thin with too many jobs. She'll fall behind in her studies."

Vanessa offered, "Maybe she can manage to use the library to study for the next few months. I want to look into getting more shifts at work to help her out."

Reggie cautioned her on this notion. "That is not what she asked for," he said. "She doesn't want you to overdo it either. You know she would want to earn her way herself. And even if you added a few shifts here and there, it wouldn't be enough." He sighed and added, "I'll call her tomorrow and let her know it's not possible."

Adult Child Viewpoint

Shanice felt hopeful after meeting with her parents. She was pleased with herself for being so organized and well prepared for the discussion. She'd found a few apartments she might be able to afford and was sure that one of them would be available. But her parents never talked about their own finances with her, and she had to admit to herself that she didn't know which way things would go.

Strategy Breakdown

Healthy communication sometimes means breaking bad news to your child; in fact, applying healthy communication is especially important in such circumstances. You don't want to make a difficult situation worse with miscommunication. Remember that you're the parent of a mature young adult who is old enough to understand that you have limitations, no matter how helpful you want to be. Honesty, respect, and clear boundaries go a long way toward cushioning disappointment. Here's how Reggie and Vanessa handled their challenging conversation with their daughter.

Maintaining a united front. Reggie wanted to call Shanice that evening, but Vanessa didn't think it was a good idea for just one of them to follow up. "It's not all on you, honey," said Vanessa. "I'd like it if we could talk to her together. This is a family decision." Respectful adult communication means both of you should take responsibility for jointly made decisions. A gentle but united front conveys you both are on the same page and trust your child to handle that.

Creating a warm and inviting setting. Money talk can quickly escalate into uncomfortable territory. Having these conversations over dinner or in another familiar setting can help bring ease to all involved. Vanessa and Reggie considered inviting Shanice to another dinner but decided not to, concerned that a dinner would seem like a special occasion and increase her disappointment. Instead, they planned a video chat, a method they often used to catch up with Shanice during her busy week. If things went badly, Shanice would be able to break away and have privacy to manage any hurt feelings.

Getting right to the point. Reggie and Vanessa knew better than to lecture their daughter—a key strategy for respectful conversation. They saw no need for speechifying about financial responsibility or goal-setting; Shanice was an adult who knew all about these things. They demonstrated their respect for her by explaining the situation directly and honestly.

Vanessa began the video chat, saying, "Listen, I know you've been waiting for an answer, and we've been looking at our finances." Reggie chimed in: "It's tough, but we just don't think we're going to be able to do this for you, Shanice. It's not that we don't trust you, but plans can go wrong and we can't risk hurting our credit." Her parents' directness, demonstrating their realistic attitude toward their own finances, provided Shanice with healthy modeling.

De-escalating conflict. Vanessa could see from Shanice's expression that she was feeling frustrated. She stepped back in to make repairs. "It's not bad that you asked, honey," she said, counteracting the bad news with positive statements. "It makes sense that you want your own place. Your dad and I are so glad you want to focus on school. We just don't have enough money coming in to float you if you run short."

Shanice felt crushed, but she could tell her parents cared and wanted to help, thanks to their healthy communication skills. "Okay," she told them, "I understand what you're saying. I'm pretty disappointed, but if you can't do it, you can't. Thanks for thinking it over."

Tips to Remember

» **Be authentic.** Share your complicated, contradictory emotions. Allow your child to see that you, too, feel vulnerable.

» **Encourage initiative.** Affirm your young adult for coming to you, even if you can't grant their request. Pointing out the positive strengthens their ability to confide in you in the future.

» **Emphasize what you can do.** Offer a compromise, partial assistance, or any other contribution you can give.

» **Affirm the validity of your child's request.** Using active listening techniques (see page 14), let them know you agree that they have a legitimate concern or that you understand why they want something to change.

» **Make sure they know you are on their side.** Whether or not you can help in any tangible way, demonstrate your caring attitude and willingness to listen.

Potential Pitfalls

This section provides examples of some common responses to an adult child that miss the opportunity to help them learn how to make thoughtful financial decisions. Then, as a comparison, consider the better approach favored by Vanessa and Reggie.

Instead of being ambiguous:

> "We're going to have to think about it some more."

> "Now's just not a good time."

Be clear:

> "We won't be able to do this for you."

Instead of being authoritarian:

> "We decided not to."

> "Because I say so."

Be collaborative:

> "We've been looking at our finances and here's why we can't do this."

Instead of blaming:

> "You know I would, but your mother said no."

> "Your dad never gives me any money either."

Take responsibility:

> "We just don't have enough money coming in to float you if you come up short."

Instead of discouraging:

> "This isn't going anywhere, so you can forget about it."

> "There's not enough money. That's all there is to it."

Be hopeful:

> "It makes sense that you want your own place. Your dad and I are so glad you want to focus on school."

Steps toward Reconnection

If financial issues have led to your young adult pulling away, a mix of empathy and honesty can help bridge the gap. Here's some language to try:

EMPATHY STATEMENTS:

I know this situation is disappointing.

I wish we could take care of this problem for you.

Believe me, if we could, we would.

HONESTY STATEMENTS:

We're still building our credit back after paying off those medical bills.

I haven't had a raise in years, and we're still only making our payments; not much is left over.

We resolved not to use credit cards anymore. Cash and checks work best for us.

Hand Out, Foot Down

"Sorry bud, your card isn't going through."

Ben had planned to grab a couple of packs of smokes and a six-pack. But it turned out he had maxed out all his cards. He'd have to hit up his parents for some cash. With nothing at home to eat but breakfast cereal, he didn't have much choice.

Hopping back in his truck, he texted, "hey mom i cd use a lil $ r u home." Ben worked as an exterior/interior specialist with the carpenters' union and was currently living on unemployment, as he usually did in the winter. Money was always tight this time of year, but this season he had big payments on his new Toyota, plus he'd replaced a bunch of his snowboarding gear. His phone buzzed: "idk lets talk sys."

At the house, Ben greeted his mom, April, with a gleaming smile and a bear hug. "What's it like being the cutest mom ever?" April laughed and pushed him playfully away. "Benny, don't you start with me," she said. "You already told me you have an ulterior motive. What's going on?"

He shrugged. "I was in the neighborhood and thought I'd swing by. I stopped to get you a surprise on the way, opened my wallet, and realized I'm short 'til payday. So how are you set for cash then, Mom? Got a hundred, couple hundred you can spare?"

April paused. "I know cute and funny has always been your thing, son," she said. "And goodness knows, it's hard for me to say no. You could charm the birds right out of the trees. But trying to sweet-talk money from your old parents?"

Ben was taken aback. "Well, no," he stammered, "not if it's going to cause you a hardship. You know I appreciate you and Dad. I didn't mean any harm in asking."

Scenario Analysis

Ben was used to skating by in life. At age 35, though, his strategy of getting through everything with the least possible effort was going to keep him in perpetual childhood. Fortunately, he had landed an excellent job, thanks to his carpentry skills. And with his easygoing personality, he was well-liked, even indulged, by most people who knew him. April was starting to see him as her lost child, though. He didn't show any signs of moving on toward getting his own house, securing a serious relationship, or pursuing any life goals.

Parent Viewpoint

April let the awkward silence sit for a couple of beats. She wasn't used to pushing back this way with Ben. The last time she gave Ben money, she and her husband, Pete, had argued about it and had both agreed a different approach was needed. Ben's brothers had moved on in life and both had a lot of responsibilities. Ben seemed like he was never going to amount to anything.

April felt she had gotten Ben's attention at the right time. Maybe this situation had opened up a chance for the kind of serious conversation he would normally not tolerate.

Adult Child Viewpoint

"I guess I put my foot in it," Ben was thinking. "Time to dash and come back another day." When Ben felt chastised, his strategy was to disappear and wait until things blew over. He'd come up with some other way to bankroll himself for the rest of the week. "Well, I guess I'd better go," he told his mother. "I'll figure this out on my own, don't you worry."

Strategy Breakdown

Parenting is often a balancing act. It's important to acknowledge that today's young adults operate under a different set of economic and financial pressures than you did at their age and may need more time to find their feet. But it's equally true that for them to transition into adulthood, you both need to move out of the caregiver-dependent relationship you're so used to. Ultimately, they'll be better off when they establish their own independent status.

Instead of acting angry at Ben's latest cash grab, April opted to change their usual dynamic. She began talking to him in a stern way he wasn't used to. Here's how April used healthy communication to nudge Ben out of his usual complacency about his finances.

Affirming competence. In chapter 2 you read that conversation beats lecturing and suggestions work better than commands (see page 13). April felt like giving Ben a piece of her mind about how he handled his money. He expected her to bail him out yet again? When was he ever going to grow up? But she remembered the discussions she'd had with her husband: We're the ones who taught him to act this way by always giving in.

"Oh, don't run off," she said to Ben. "If you help us get some projects out of the way, we can pay you, no problem." She gestured toward a kitchen cabinet door that was practically fallen off its hinges. "There's a bunch of loose ends around this place, and your dad is too proud to admit it, but he could really use an experienced carpenter."

Outlining expectations. Setting boundaries requires clear expectations. April listed a few of the tasks that needed doing. She made it clear that they would pay for materials and for Ben's time. But he'd have to come through with his commitment. She was surprised at how easily the words came to her once she got started. *Maybe I should have put my foot down with this one a long time ago*, April thought.

Relying on values for guidance. Even though it satisfied her urge to be generous to her children, April believed parents should raise their kids with a good work ethic. Family members should help each other. She wanted to feel proud of and respect all her sons. From now on, she would take a firm stance when Ben asked for a handout.

Potential Pitfalls

When money's tight—and when isn't it?—discussions can become arguments quickly. This section provides some knee-jerk reactions to requests for money and follow-ups with the more constructive ways of expressing legitimate concerns.

Instead of criticizing:

"All you think about is yourself."

Try expressing vulnerability:

"It's hurtful that we don't seem to hear from you until you need something. I'd like it if you'd keep in touch more often."

Instead of accusing:

"You earn good money, what did you do with it this time?"

Try giving feedback:

"I'm concerned that you're running out of cash before payday. What's causing that?"

Instead of name-calling:

"You're nothing but a spoiled brat."

Try stepping away:

> "I think it would be better to try talking about this later, I'm getting upset."

Instead of shaming:

> "You've never been any good with money."

Try offering encouragement:

> "I bet you can figure it out. If you're really in a jam, let me know and we can talk again. Your dad and I believe in you. It's rough now, but it'll get better."

Tips to Remember

» **Offer respect.** To get respect, show respect. Even if your adult child still ignites your temper, maintain self-control. Hold to a respectful tone as well as respectful words and body language; resist the pull of any troubled history you share.

» **Be the change.** Most of us spend too much time wishing we could change other people. You can start changing patterns in your family anytime by starting to behave differently yourself. It won't necessarily be easy, but instead of waiting for someone else to change, initiate change through your actions.

» **Remember your values.** We'll talk about values next, in chapter 5; you are continually demonstrating your values to your children. Consider what you believe about right, moral, and correct behavior, and put your ideas into action. Your children may disagree, but they will admire you for holding firm to your principles.

Steps toward Reconnection

Young adults who struggle with money may drift away from their family because of shame, resentment, or, as in Ben's case, a retreat from responsibility. April pre-empted this tendency by acknowledging his strengths (charm, carpentry skills) and briskly giving a directive, telling him to help around their house. Affirming to the adult child that their family needs them and that they have an important role can reassure the adult child that their worth is not defined by their financial successes or failures.

Reflection Questions

» Do you think a person's finances should always be kept private? Is it better for the generations to talk openly about one another's money situations?

» What aspects of your own financial life might cause resentment or envy within the family?

» If you have siblings, do you discuss financial matters with them? What are the ground rules?

» Do you have any financial secrets from anyone?

» What financial lessons or habits do you want to make sure your children learn from you?

Chapter 5

Differences in Values

We live with assumptions or values that seem right to us because they're the basis of everything we know. Like the air we breathe, these values are not something we stop to think about every day, which helps explain why conflicts over values ask a lot of us. We find ourselves asked to question beliefs and emotions we don't usually examine. Some degree of disagreement over core values is inevitable as young adults break away and establish themselves. But keep in mind that there's probably more common ground between you than you think.

The Glove That Didn't Fit

Perry and Donna had traveled across the country to visit their grandson, Forrest, for his 11th birthday. When they arrived, Forrest jumped up and down with excitement. Eventually they all settled down to enjoy lunch together.

When Forrest opened his birthday gift from Grandma and Grandpa, his animated expression suddenly turned blank, and he glanced over at his father, Daniel, in silent confusion.

"Are you excited, kiddo?" asked Perry. "That's an auto-graphed Andrew Benintendi glove. Do you follow the Red Sox? When you visit us next year, we can go to the Baseball Hall of Fame!"

Forrest didn't reply. "Ah, Dad, thank you so much," said Daniel, half-heartedly breaking the silence. "That is a really awe-some, thoughtful gift. I'll be glad to play catch with Forrest."

Meanwhile, Forrest pushed the gift aside. He didn't even take the glove out of the box. "Mom!" he whined, "I asked for the new Sims! Didn't you get me that?" His mom, Mandy, wasn't concealing her own annoyance. "Forrest, it's not time now," she finally said. "We have company. I'm saving it for later." Without thinking, she muttered to Perry and Donna, "He has really different interests, but thank you."

Perry saw that his big gift had failed to produce the thrill he expected. "What is this?" he demanded of Daniel. "I thought this would be a big hit. I spent a lot of money on that glove." He looked deflated.

Scenario Analysis

Perry and Donna wanted to connect with their grandson. Because they lived far away, they didn't often see him. Based on their assumptions about what would appeal to a child his age, they thought they were bringing Forrest something extra special that he would love. But Perry and Donna hadn't accounted for changing customs of children. They also had not confirmed the gift with Forrest's parents, so they were not current on his tastes and interests.

Parent Viewpoint

Perry was offended and frustrated. He was just trying to give the kid a present. In his mind, any normal boy would be expected to get an autographed baseball glove. It was a collector's item. Daniel had loved baseball growing up. How could he not have passed that interest along to his son? Perry was angry and embarrassed to have his gift spurned. Both Daniel and Mandy seemed to be taking the child's side when they should have chastised him for being rude to his grandparents.

Adult Child Viewpoint

Daniel hated to see his dad hurt this way. But what kind of giant misunderstanding had happened that he had taken this baseball thing so far? Perry and Donna hadn't seen Forrest for several years, and they didn't really keep up the relationship. Why would they assume they knew what Forrest was interested in?

Meanwhile, Mandy was trying to keep Forrest's birthday from being ruined. He'd move past the disappointment of the gift fairly quickly; he was eleven. But even if he didn't pick up on exactly what was going on among the adults, he likely sensed the mood shift. She didn't want what happened to become a bad memory for him.

Strategy Breakdown

When values clash, the topic feels deeply personal. That's true not only for the convictions that guide our lives but for less significant preferences, like favoring baseball or computer games. When someone we love rejects aspects of our life that don't seem like a big deal on the surface, we can nevertheless feel belittled. Here are the practices Perry and Donna used to rebound from the incident:

Manage defensiveness. There was more to Perry's discomfort than a show of generosity falling flat. He believed that sports, specifically team sports, held essential lessons for personal development. He and Donna shared the value that children should learn manners and make a show of appreciation, even if the gift is not what they would have chosen. Forrest spurning their present was a sign he wasn't raised this way. As they unpacked, Donna helped Perry recognize he was being defensive. She reminded him of the importance of using this time to reconnect with their distant family.

"Don't let this rocky start to the visit derail your relationship with your son and grandson," she told him. They decided to join the family again on the back patio.

Make repairs. "I'll take a beer. Thanks, son," Perry responded to Daniel's offer. The small moment of appreciation helped change the mood. Donna asked brightly, "Are there more presents Forrest can open?" Her question put the group's attention back on the reason for their gathering. Although she wasn't feeling terrific, Donna demonstrated with her question that she was willing to try to make things feel better for everyone.

Refrain from blame. Donna reminded herself they had not been to visit in a while, so it shouldn't be surprising they didn't really know what interested Forrest these days. And he was just a child; it wasn't his fault the gifts they chose were not right for him. Finger-pointing wouldn't undo what was really just an honest mistake. She made a mental note to check gift ideas with Daniel beforehand next time.

Potential Pitfalls

It's wise to tread carefully when an unexpected clash of values erupts. Avoid these behaviors, which tend to throw fuel on the fire:

Staging a debate. Aggressive arguing can lead to anger and hurtful words. It would not have been helpful for Perry to continue giving reasons why he thought his birthday gift was terrific. Instead, he stopped talking and dealt with his frustration, which allowed everyone else to collect themselves and refocus.

Standing on a soapbox. Neither he nor Donna did any lecturing or criticizing. Even though they had their own thoughts about Forrest and how his parents were raising him, they knew it was not for them to say.

Seeking an audience. Donna and Perry agreed with each other that they'd deal with their complicated emotions about family by themselves. Although there might be momentary satisfaction in venting to other family members, they knew doing so could make matters worse.

Tips to Remember

» **Manage your expectations.** When families live far apart, there's pressure for each occasion to be a flawless and memorable experience. It helps to maintain realistic expectations.

» **Rely on self-care.** Sometimes a clash of values is especially draining or painful. Practicing self-care—meditating or getting outside for a vigorous walk—helps manage stress.

» **Keep the group in mind.** Donna tried to show a caring and interested attitude, even during an awkward exchange. Prioritizing the needs of the group over your own is essential to family functioning.

Steps toward Reconnection

Everyone's values change with age and as life experiences accumulate. If the parent and adult child drift apart over the years, tracking those changes becomes harder for both the parent and adult child. Rather than jump to conclusions, allow your child's actions to demonstrate what matters to them. Share your own dilemmas and confusions with them so they can deepen their understanding of how you've changed over time.

The New Son-in-Law

Marla was winding down her weekend and about to finish cleaning up her email inbox in preparation for Monday morning. A message appeared from her daughter Tabitha; since they talked frequently, it was unusual for Tabby to bother using email. Marla opened the message and read:

Dear Mom,

I have some news and thought it would be good to send you a note, so you have time to think this over before the next time we talk. I wanted to let you know Kelly and I have been making some changes that may affect the family.

You and I haven't discussed this before, but Kelly told me a few years ago that he is bisexual. We have been talking openly about this for a long time, and in the last couple of years, we agreed to open our marriage. We wanted everything to be honest and we intend to stay married.

People think Dominic is Kelly's new best friend. He has actually become our partner. We're now a triad, or some people call it a "thruple." Since Dominic spends most of his time at our place already, we're making preparations for him to move in with us.

I know this is a lot to think about. I'm telling you all this because you will be seeing more of him on our social media, and we want to include him in our life. We have already taken a few trips and a vacation together, and we're starting to plan to spend the holidays together.

Mom, I'm very excited and I would love to share this chapter of our life with you, but I'm not really sure what else to say right now. I hope you will be able to accept this and get to know another new son-in-law. Let me know when you're ready to talk things over.

Much love,
Tab

Marla felt hot and queasy, and had to reread the message several times. What could Tabitha be thinking? How did they keep this situation under wraps for so long? She thought she was close with her daughter, and all along, she had been carrying on some kind of . . . what? Affair? Fling? She hadn't raised her daughter this way . . . What were people going to think of her family? Marla shut down the computer and took a bath. She tossed and turned when she got to bed and barely slept that night.

Scenario Analysis

The news hit Marla hard—to call it unexpected was an understatement. She was in shock. Tabitha's life choices did not align with her mother's ideals. This new information put both women on the defense. Marla, in particular, felt her own values of monogamy, along with her assumptions about proper behavior in marriage, being challenged. She tried to keep an open mind, wanting to understand Tabitha's point of view.

Parent Viewpoint

Marla couldn't comprehend what Tabitha was telling her. A marriage with two husbands was preposterous. Marla herself had divorced after Tabitha's father had an affair with a co-worker. And now Tabitha was tolerating unfaithfulness? Marla adored Kelly, yet now she had to cope with the fact that her daughter's husband had a secret life. It was all just too much.

Marla considered herself an open-minded person. On the other hand, this knowledge created an uncomfortable portal into her daughter's intimate life that Marla really would rather not have known about. More than anything, hearing that they had all been keeping this illicit secret from her hurt the most. She thought what they were doing was immoral and probably illegal, at least somewhere. But she didn't like being left out of things and feeling like a fool.

Adult Child Viewpoint

Tabitha had given a lot of thought to how to tell her mom about this aspect of her life. She anticipated a big reaction. She, Kelly, and Dominic were tired of hiding things and keeping up the pretense of a monogamous marriage. They felt they shouldn't have to hide the truth, at least from people they were close to. If they couldn't be honest about it with their own families, what did that say about their relationships with them?

Tabitha felt like she was chickening out by informing Marla over email; she didn't want to cause distress for her mom, but she couldn't imagine delivering the news in person. They could process the situation together after some of the shock had passed.

Strategy Breakdown

Sometimes keeping a connection with our child requires allowing them to be separate individuals. Parents can only withhold judgment and try to understand—and communicate their understanding to their children through respectful conversation and active listening. When the going gets rough, remember the power of the enduring connection you have with your child. Journal about fond memories, look through scrapbooks, and share stories with another parent; do whatever helps you reconnect with loving feelings that may have been shaken by your adult child's unexpected choices.

For Marla, *keep calm and carry on* became an important mantra as she tried to focus at work the next day. It felt to her like the rules of society had crumbled beyond all recognition. Well, she loved Tab, so they would just have to find a way to see this situation through. Marla navigated this unexpected difference between her values and her daughter's lifestyle by utilizing these strategies:

Draw strength from previous successes. Remember that, as we discussed in chapter 1 (see page 3), you're in a new phase of parenting, which means you've brought your child this far and have earned the right to trust the connection you've established. When Marla felt overwhelmed at the thought of discussing things with Tabitha, she thought back to when she first realized her daughter was using marijuana while living at home and in college. She'd employed active listening by asking questions and keeping a respectful tone (see page 14). And she'd deliberately affirmed her trust in Tabitha even though she was upset with her.

Reach out. Marla kept thinking about another principle she'd learned in her time as a younger parent: Don't be afraid to make the first move. As we saw in chapter 2, reaching out with a brief message is an effective way to stay connected with your adult child, whether during a rough patch or just to keep in touch (see page 22). In this case, Marla didn't want Tab to fret about her response while she waited to hear back. She dashed off a message:

Thanks for this unexpected update. I wanted to let you know I'm thinking about your message. Let me know when you have time to talk.

Love,
Mom

Remembering goals. In chapter 1, we discussed goals parents might have for their relationship with their children (see page 7). Marla's goal was to stay close to her daughter despite her own stirrings of uncertainty and unease around Tab's choices. Marla wasn't sure how she would conceal her distress when it came to discussing this unconventional arrangement. Talking about intimate aspects of her daughter's marriage felt overwhelmingly personal and private. She had to deal with her own messy feelings about cheating in marriage, and she still wasn't sure how to handle all of that. But her top priority of keeping connected to Tabitha overruled any temptation to avoid the issue or refuse to accept the situation.

Potential Pitfalls

We already know we're in sensitive territory when it comes to discussing values. How do we sidestep the hot spots to have productive and respectful conversations? Here are some approaches to avoid:

Judging. Marla already knew she had judgments about and reactions to Tabitha's arrangement; there was no getting around that. The best she could hope to do in a conversation was to suspend her opinions and try to learn about Tabitha's experience and perspective.

Catastrophizing. She felt panicky and afraid about what trouble this situation could lead to for the whole family, but she reminded herself that Tabitha was smart; Marla trusted her.

Lecturing. Marla wanted to alert her daughter to the big mistake she was making. She resolved if she caught that tone in her voice, she would say she needed to take a break, and they could talk more later.

Tips to Remember

Whether it's a major bombshell or minor annoyance, keep these points in mind when faced with a disparity in values between you and your adult child:

» **Remember that you're living your life and your adult child is living theirs.** Worrisome as it may be that you don't see eye to eye, your job as a parent of an adult is to step out of the way and let your child do as they see fit. Unless they're risking their life or that of someone else, you must tolerate the role of innocent bystander even if you are convinced you know better.

» **Take things slowly.** Marla had a million questions. She could easily have made a list and just fired them at her daughter. But she had to allow Tabby to set the pace of the conversation because what was happening was about Tabby's life. Marla wanted her daughter to feel in charge.

» **Expect a positive outcome.** When you have a conflict in values with your adult child, you may feel as though you will never find the bridge. If you hold on to the belief that you will eventually understand and accept each other, that conviction will help you see your way through the toughest conversations.

Steps toward Reconnection

A significant difference in values can feel like it will inevitably put distance between you and your child. But what it really means is a chance to more deeply understand the adult child you've raised. After Tabitha's revelation, Marla realized she'd missed quite a lot of Tabitha's inner thoughts and possibly complicated experiences for at least the last several years. It couldn't have been easy for her daughter to hold back the truth. Marla decided, like it or not, she wanted to catch up. True, she wanted to yell "How could you?" or "Did you have to drag me into this mess?" but she knew that wasn't fair. Her real wish was to understand the whole person she knew as Tabby.

Reflection Questions

» Which of your values are unshakable?

» What values would you say you learned in your family?

» How have you modified your values or changed your perspective on moral issues over time?

» What fundamental values do you anticipate your child, and any future generations, will absorb from you?

Chapter 6

Addiction and Substance Abuse

A 2019 analysis of data from the Centers for Disease Control showed that in the previous decade, Millennials (people born between 1981 and 1994) were more likely than any other age group to die from drugs, alcohol, or suicide. Between 2007 and 2017, deaths caused by alcohol rose by 69 percent. Drug-related deaths increased by 108 percent.

A number of factors likely contribute to this grim trend. The average education debt for young adults now exceeds $30,000. Due to unfavorable economic conditions, today's generation faces unusual difficulty starting careers. This cohort often lacks access to health care or mental health services. And families trying to provide emotional support to their troubled offspring typically operate with little-to-no financial safety net.

Crisis Call

Victor nudged Shannon out of her sleep, "Honey, wake up," he told her. "It's the ER, they're calling about Brittany. They treated her for alcohol poisoning. She told them to call us."

"What? Oh. Oh my God." Shannon shook her head to try to wake herself up as Victor got back on the phone. She listened to him converse with the ER doctor then flopped back onto the bed in frustration as he hung up. "I'm glad to know she's someplace safe," she said. "But she's almost 30 years old! How many times do we have to go through this?"

Brittany had extended periods of sobriety, but her alcohol use had caused intermittent problems since college. Her boyfriend of the past three years had recently broken up with her, so her parents knew things were rocky. Victor and Shannon always did their best to lend emotional support, yet drastic incidents would still occur.

At the ER, they learned Brittany had been talking to a crisis line staff member who called 911 when she became unresponsive. The parents agreed with the doctor's recommendation to bring her to their home.

Shannon and Victor had downsized a few years ago, so they didn't have a spare room. They bundled Brittany on the couch and went back to bed. Shannon sighed. "God, she looks just horrible. She probably doesn't have anything to eat at her apartment."

"Try to let it go until the morning," Victor said wearily. "At least she got help. We'll have a fresh start tomorrow." He began dozing; Shannon was left with her worried, repetitive thoughts.

Scenario Analysis

Brittany's parents lived with the difficult moral question of what they were obligated to provide to their adult child.

The burdens of Brittany's alcohol addiction meant they were still in the process of helping their daughter progress into full-fledged adulthood, and she would turn to them for various kinds of support and advice. There were no clear, crisp lines to delineate where they should stop their involvement. Their own parental judgment felt insufficient to guide them. They'd turned to the Internet for information and advice, but though they'd come across some nuggets of crucial information, they found their online search overall to be a bit of a maze.

Parent Viewpoint

Shannon came from a family riddled with alcoholism, and she was distraught when they first learned of Brittany's descent into problem drinking. Victor was equally concerned but always patient with Brittany. He was steadfast, and his attitude was: *Anything she needs; we're going to make sure she gets help.*

They'd received conflicting messages from counselors at treatment centers when she was younger. Some advised them to let her hit bottom, meaning reaching her lowest point, so she would be compelled to change. At times, staff had told them they were enabling Brittany, supporting her excessive drinking and, through their caretaking efforts, allowing the problem to persist. They both sporadically attended Al-Anon meetings; these gatherings would "help families and friends of problem drinkers recover from the impacts of a loved one's drinking." Shannon and Victor found some help there, but neither enjoyed group participation. They ended up going only when they felt they had to.

Adult Child Viewpoint

Brittany loved her parents and felt terrible to have caused problems and expense for them over the years. She hoped someday she would really feel "in recovery," but it was usually touch and go. She could last months without thinking much about drinking and then something would set her off; she felt as though she were sleepwalking or watching someone else live her life. When she had a partner, drinking was easier to resist because she knew they would discourage or confront her. When her boyfriend, Jesse, broke off their relationship and moved out, she had to deal with the wrenching loneliness and sense of, once again, having failed at love. Her parents were amazingly supportive but couldn't help with everything.

Strategy Breakdown

Addiction presents parents with an unusual challenge because they are trying to support their child in independence, but the child's life is out of control. There are bound to be mistakes and reversals. As you work on setting boundaries, keep in mind that doing so is a messy, trial-and-error kind of process, even for less significant matters. Having to change plans and reset expectations along the way doesn't mean you failed. Shannon and Victor moved forward after Britany's sudden turn for the worse by following these strategies:

Practice self-care. Shannon, feeling particularly upset at seeing her daughter in this state again, was determined to do something to take care of herself this week. Her goal was to get to an Al-Anon meeting. She'd been attending these gatherings on and off for most of her life. Knowing that other ordinary people were holding a similar experience of suffering always brought her some relief during a crisis. Seeing that they, too, were good people trying their best helped Shannon be gentler with herself.

Validate and encourage. Shannon knew she needed to remain supportive of Brittany without taking charge of her life. Besides helping Brittany set up a doctor's appointment, she offered to go with her to the appointment, just like she would do with any other kind of illness. She wanted not only to support Brittany in whatever efforts she was willing to make but also to treat her as an adult by following her lead.

Avoid blame. Brittany's parents knew that professionals could help Brittany handle her addiction, but that they, too, had a part to play. Even if she made progress, Brittany was going to need their help for a long time. Resenting Brittany for all the hardship they were undergoing would have been easy, but Shannon and Victor made a pact: If either of them expressed blame toward Brittany in a moment of frustration, the other would gently correct them.

Potential Pitfalls

If addiction is an issue for you and your adult child, do your best to avoid these bad communication habits:

Mis-timing your efforts. Before initiating a discussion or making a request, assess the situation and determine whether your child is capable of fruitful participation.

Example: Brittany's parents learned not to talk to Brittany about her drinking when she was under the influence or recovering from a binge. These conversations just ended up being wasted energy and caused Brittany to get defensive.

Ignoring immediate needs. Of course the big picture is important, but an urgent problem sometimes needs to be handled first to avoid further disaster. When dealing with an acute addiction flare-up, consider what practical support or problem-solving will allow you and your child to get through the day or week.

Example: In the past, Shannon and Victor had tried letting Brittany deal with the consequences of a drinking binge on her own. But losing her job was too significant a price to pay and would make her recovery much harder. This time, they rehearsed a phone call with Brittany so she could arrange two days of sick time, then helped plan her return to work.

Trying to assume control. Offer a steadfast presence instead of imposing your will on your adult child.

Example: Victor and Shannon knew they could not control their adult daughter by taking away her keys or phone, telling her what to do, forbidding contact with anyone, or otherwise treating her like a teenager. These draconian methods would fail and prompt Brittany not to be honest with them going forward. Instead, they emphasized that they were a resource for her and would help as requested.

Tips to Remember

» **Maintain a peer relationship.** As you educate yourself about addiction, share information with your child. Communicate that you are a fellow seeker, trying to make sense of the situation as their ally and not an authority who will dictate the answers to problems.

» **Find the right kind of support for yourself.** You are the judge of what types of self-care are best for you. Groups and gatherings, for example, are nourishing for some and draining for others. Show your child they can identify and customize the activities that fit best for them as well.

Steps toward Reconnection

The pressures of dealing with addiction make managing your self-care especially important. Doing so will allow you to gain the inner resources needed to reestablish damaged relationships. Having a go-to strategy to call on when you feel overwhelmed can be helpful. As one example, many people are familiar with the "Serenity Prayer," a touchstone for the Twelve Step movement originating with Alcoholics Anonymous and attributed to theologian Reinhold Neibuhr:

God grant me the serenity to accept the things I cannot change, courage to change the things I can, and wisdom to know the difference.

If prayer does not appeal to you, consider other methods, like meditating, listening to calming music, reciting a favorite poem, taking a walk, or spending some time outdoors.

Aiding Aidan

Aidan stopped by to see his parents. It was time to let somebody know he was not doing well.

"Mom?" he called as he let himself in the back door. Tammy was startled as she walked into the kitchen. Aidan hadn't been responding to messages for several weeks, and she had been concerned. "Oh, sweetie, you startled me," she exclaimed. "Where have you been? We've been trying to reach you."

Aidan's dad, Scott, came in and exclaimed, "Aidan! You don't look too good. You okay?" Tammy saw that Aidan had lost quite a bit of weight.

Aidan was autistic and lived by himself. Years ago, Tammy and Scott had helped him qualify for disability, and he eventually moved into subsidized housing. He kept himself busy with volunteering and video games. He was an avid user of the public library and loved listening to vintage jazz.

Aidan explained he had been given pain medicine after dental surgery last month. The relaxed feeling from the pain killers was terrific. Even though he didn't need them anymore, he bought some pills online. Now he was craving the opiate. He wasn't eating and he felt dizzy and had an upset stomach.

His parents let Aidan know they were glad he had come to them for help. Scott said, "Aidan, I think you need to call the doctor tomorrow. Is that what you were planning?"

Aidan answered, "I'm embarrassed to call. I shouldn't have bought any of this stuff. It was so stupid."

"Well, we can talk about what led up to it later, but right now, this is a medical problem," Tammy said. "The doctor's job is not to judge you." She offered to him that he could stay overnight. "That way you can make the call from here in the morning. I can help you write down what to say, if you like."

Scenario Analysis

Aidan's support needs had decreased over time. He had stable housing and managed his schedule and self-care routines. His parents would check in with him occasionally, but they felt little urgency if they had not heard from him for a while. He was a creature of habit who enjoyed his routine and liked to keep to himself. They encouraged his independence and, for the most part, felt their role was to respect his privacy. Now they were wondering if they needed to rethink their decision.

Parent Viewpoint

This incident had Scott thinking about how he only had wanted to protect Aidan from harm when his son was little. Those feelings were still there, but Scott knew he couldn't shield his son from the stresses and demands of adult life. Scott felt his own role was to work hard and earn as much as possible so he and Tammy would continue having resources they needed for Aidan's care. They all wished there were more options for Aidan, but until now, his situation had seemed relatively stable and safe.

Adult Child Viewpoint

The pain and worry wore Aidan down. He hadn't slept well in about a month, which he found alarming because he knew he needed to keep to a routine. He was scared of being addicted; he liked to be in control of himself. He felt uncomfortable confiding in his parents about this secret, but at least he knew he could count on them for help.

Aidan didn't like the building where he lived and only stayed because it was all he could afford. Some of the other residents were loud and unpredictable. They said weird things and directed strange remarks and questions to him. He overheard stories about robberies in the building and didn't feel entirely safe. That medicine had given him a deep calm he hadn't experienced before, but now it had just led to trouble. Hopefully the doctor would have some answers. He had already searched for help online and had some ideas about getting off the drugs.

Strategy Breakdown

Parents who've never dealt with addiction before will likely have many questions to ask and plenty of concern to express when this behavior becomes an issue with their adult child. But when your child comes to you with an addiction issue, remember to stick to the communication strategies of asking before giving advice and conversing rather than lecturing (see pages 15 and 17). Someone coping with symptoms of addiction or withdrawal or who's burdened by the anxiety or stress of managing the condition can easily be overwhelmed if pushed to share more information than they can handle. Tammy and Scott applied their parenting skills to their son's situation following these methods:

Employ active listening. Aidan's parents already knew the best way to support their son in difficult situations was to let him explain his immediate plans to deal with the problem, asking open-ended questions as needed. In this case, Aidan already had ideas about how he wanted to approach this issue. Tammy pushed to accompany him to the doctor's office, but he balked. "Mom," he told her, "I already feel like a loser. I don't even know if they let an adult bring someone in the office with them." Tammy reflected his statement back to him, showing that she understood. "Of course, you're an adult, you don't want to seem like you need your mother to come with you to the doctor's."

Set clear expectations. As usual, Aidan didn't mince words. Scott and Tammy were used to that, but in this situation, his blunt refusal was concerning to them. They shared their concerns and let Aidan know that they'd leave him to it but expected him to arrive at the appointment prepared so he could get clear guidance from the doctor. Since Aidan was easily flustered at doctor's appointments, he agreed to compose a statement, with their help, about his problem that he could read to the doctor if needed.

Affirm good judgment. Aidan did emerge from his appointment the next afternoon with some answers and a plan, and Scott and Tammy were relieved. They let him know they were impressed with how he had handled the doctor's appointment and that he had shared the results with them.

Potential Pitfalls

Addiction comes with all sorts of stigmas and cultural baggage that can make communicating with your adult child harder. Avoid these behaviors so you can focus on the problems at hand:

Reacting with high-drama. Of course this kind of situation is likely to leave you feeling upset, alarmed, even frightened. Do your best to modulate your reactions to avoid overstimulating or overwhelming your child and exacerbating their distress. If your emotions get the better of you, rely on your conflict management techniques to de-escalate (see page 18).

Criticizing, blaming, and saying "I told you so." Your child is likely doing more than enough self-criticism already.

Tips to Remember

» **Respect autonomy.** Tammy and Scott avoided taking over for Aidan, instead offering options and allowing him to guide his treatment plan. If they had thought he needed feedback, they would have stepped in, but they wanted to encourage his willingness to interact with medical professionals on his own so that he could learn to advocate for himself.

» **Reevaluate needs.** Even though they wanted to preserve his independence, Aidan's parents realized this incident was a signal that Aidan wasn't managing as capably as he had been. They requested he keep regular check-in times with them as he progressed through his treatment. He agreed with their request to go back to an old agreement: If he did not respond to his parents' messages, his parents had his permission to get the building's resident coordinator to knock on his door to make sure he was okay.

Steps toward Reconnection

An addiction-related scare can make parents feel they need to return to a caretaker role. But an adult who's struggling with addiction is still an adult. Discuss options with your child rather than try to dictate them. Aidan's parents planned more frequent contact with him and would renegotiate the details periodically. Aidan agreed to document his participation in recovery meetings for accountability to his parents. As they looked back on other episodes when Aidan had had difficulties, they came to view the current incident as a temporary adjustment, not a failure or setback.

Reflection Questions

Nearly half of the U.S. population has a friend or family member with alcohol or drug problems. Here are some questions to ponder if addiction is part of your relationship with an adult child:

» How has addiction touched your life or that of someone close to you? Do you think most people are aware of the extent of the addiction problem in today's society?

» How would you have approached the adult children in this chapter? Do you see missed opportunities where the parents could have done anything differently?

» What added complications are present when someone with a lifelong developmental disability deals with addiction? How are families uniquely positioned to help?

Chapter 7

High-Conflict Situations

Conflict is not necessarily destructive. The way your family handles disagreements depends on everyone's ability to tolerate the free expression of emotion. Families vary widely in this arena. Airing out differences can be done with a formal approach—some families prefer meeting around the dining room table, for example, when there is a problem. Others communicate in less direct ways with family members interpreting one another's feelings or carrying messages among those involved to avoid awkward exchanges or heated emotions.

Stereotypes portray Italians yelling over each other or Midwesterners being overly polite. There are all kinds of family dynamics, and cultural tendencies may play a part as well. However, all styles of handling emotion can work well in families, and as long as nobody behaves abusively, people can manage well together despite challenging conflicts.

Restaurant Row

The Embers restaurant had been in business for over 30 years, ever since Aahad and Rashida fled war in Lebanon to start a new life in the United States. Their sons, Masab and Farez, had grown up in the business, doing homework at the tables and fetching napkins and silverware for the servers. Masab, the older son, always felt like the restaurant was a home away from home; he was grateful to have work he enjoyed that connected him to his community.

Farez recently began taking classes at community college and had not been pulling his weight. Tension had arisen between Masab and Farez. Rashida asked Masab about it during an afternoon lull at the restaurant. "It's absolutely becoming a problem, yes," said Masab. "I had to cover two of his shifts with hardly any notice. I'm getting fed up." Rashida was taken aback at how upset he was. "I didn't know it was that bad," she said. "Do you want your dad to talk to him?"

Masab seemed to get even angrier at the question. "No, I don't want to get Dad involved! I thought it was up to me to run this place now. You're getting ready to retire and the way things are going, it's all going to be my responsibility! I never got to choose for myself. He's the baby, and you've always indulged him. That's just the way it is."

Rashida tried to calm him, saying, "Wait, I thought you loved the business. You're always so happy when your friends show up. You talk about how much you love hosting people and making everybody happy with beautiful food."

"Don't you get it? I had to love the restaurant. I didn't have choices because you and Dad would just tell me, 'We can't afford that' or 'That's not a real job.' You wouldn't ever buy me anything new, but you've set him up with all this expensive camera equipment for his film classes." Masab glared at her for a moment and then stormed off, going out back to have a smoke.

Scenario Analysis

Family businesses tend to be either prosperous and stable or a breeding ground for temper and high drama. Living with such continuous contact and interdependence is challenging. Fears about financial security, fair treatment, and whether work is equitably shared get stirred up and need to be resolved.

In this scenario, we see how old emotional themes can reverberate from the past, with sibling rivalries feeling quite vivid between the adult children. Also, the line between career and home becomes blurred, so all waking hours can get taken up with work-related tasks and conversations.

Parent Viewpoint

Rashida didn't want bad feelings to fester between her sons. She knew she was taking a risk bringing up the issue but hadn't realized how intensely Masab was feeling mistreated or unappreciated. It was shocking to see him so angry. He had practically shouted at her.

Rashida felt as though the ground was shifting underneath her feet. *What kind of life did he want?* she wondered. She had always seen Masab as part of the family business. Was he rejecting it now after his parents' lifetime of hard work and sacrifice? Masab had worked hard, too. Maybe they had asked too much of him. She felt sad and confused and realized her eyes were starting to tear up.

Adult Child Viewpoint

Masab tried to calm down while he had a cigarette. He usually kidded around with the kitchen staff before the evening rush, but today he was in no mood.

He didn't recall ever talking so sharply to his mom before. He'd taken things too far. But maybe she needed to hear the truth. Nobody had ever asked him what he wanted and now

Farez was flaking out and leaving Masab to deal with all the family business problems. He felt overwhelmed.

Masab went back inside and found his mother. "Mom, I apologize," he said to her. "I'm sorry. That was disrespectful. We'd better get back to work. Let's meet for lunch tomorrow. I'd like to make it up to you."

Strategy Breakdown

Family secrets can be bombshells. When conflict flares up and reveals new, perhaps long-hidden information, conflict management skills can create space for you to process what's been said before heightened emotions lead to a serious fracture in the relationship. If you've been knocked for a loop and don't know how to react, de-escalate the situation. Avoid blame, control your own defensiveness, and break away so you can consider the most constructive way to respond. Afterward, try to conduct a respectful conversation in order to get the whole story.

Rashida wanted to help Masab, but she knew taking sides in the tension between the brothers wouldn't work. She also didn't want to give him the impression she thought he wasn't capable of managing the relationship with Farez. Rashida used these communication skills to gain a better understanding of the situation:

Asking open-ended questions. The next day Rashida waited for Masab to return to the conversation from the previous day. When he kept talking about everyday matters, she prompted him, saying, "I'd like to hear more about what you were saying yesterday."

"I'm sorry, Mom," he said. "I was tired. I shouldn't shoot off at the mouth like that."

"I wonder what else you would want me to know about your thoughts these days?" She spoke gently and gave him time to consider her questions.

Masab shrugged. "There's nothing you can do about it. We just have to all keep going and working as hard as we can."

Engage in active listening and reflecting emotions. Rashida sensed her son was close to opening up. She signaled she was here to listen. "Well, still," said Rashida. "You sound unhappy. What can be done? Do you also want to go to school?"

Masab looked frustrated. "Mom, that isn't what this is about. It's just, where was all this support you're giving Farez when I was younger? I remember I was interested in pro skateboarding, but I had to teach myself on that piece of junk we got at Walmart. Then I wanted to be a game designer or do graphic design. You told me those weren't practical ideas. So, I never let myself think about anything except the restaurant. And now, here we are."

Converse as equals. Rashida felt stung but reminded herself to breathe and keep listening. Her son was sharing something personal and she didn't want to shut down the conversation, painful as it was. She also wanted to provide some background on how she and Aahad had made decisions. He was an adult who could understand these things.

"Okay," she said, "I can tell you some of what was behind that. Farez, of course, is younger than you, by seven years, so you grew up in very different circumstances. We struggled when you were a kid. We honestly didn't have much money back then." She continued, "It's not too late for you to do other things. You can be an artist now if that's what you want. We could talk about selling the business. Are you interested in that?"

Potential Pitfalls

Navigating a high-conflict situation with your adult child requires proceeding with caution. Beware of scenarios that could derail your progress, such as:

Trying to fix the problem. Solutions rarely come easily in situations like this one; to imply otherwise is to imply that you're not hearing how much pain the other party is feeling. When Rashida realized that instead of listening to Masab, as she had resolved to do, she had jumped into trying to solve the problem, she stopped talking to allow him time to respond.

"That's not the point," Masab responded. "I wanted support. You and Dad were working so much, the only way I could get your attention was to join the restaurant crew. I never had a chance to choose anything else."

Comparing grievances. Statements like "It was hard for me, too" or "It's painful for me to hear this" puts your own emotions in the spotlight. As much as you can, focus on the other person's feelings and employ emotional reflection. "It must have been hard to have us so caught up in work," Rashida told Masab. "I'm sure it felt as though we had no time for you."

Tips to Remember

» **Conflict is challenging.** Being a parent to an adult is an entirely different experience from raising children. It requires a different skill set and will challenge you at new levels.

» **Listening helps healing.** As she anticipated their conversation, Rashida had to keep reminding herself Masab was looking for empathy from her. He was talking about childhood needs but from an adult vantage point. Her role was not to share her perspective but to listen.

» **Risks are worth taking.** It may feel scary to get to the root of things, but ignoring a conflict can lead to resentment and separation. Rashida could have avoided Masab's sour mood and accepted what he had said as irritation. Instead, she reached beneath the surface of what he said to learn more about what was behind his words.

» **Honesty is compelling.** Give your adult child your real understanding of their situation. If you need to venture a guess or say something gently, doing so is worth trying. Sometimes truthfulness is overwhelming and needs to come in small doses.

Steps toward Reconnection

Rashida knew she couldn't give Masab back his childhood. Instead, she murmured, "I wish it had been different." Masab reached for her hand and said, "Me too, Mom. Me too." You (probably) don't have a magic wand you can wave to change the past and make your child's wishes come true. But expressing the idea can be a powerful unifying force, showing your child that you're on their side.

Dressed for the Weather

The multi-generational celebration was well underway and Scarlett strolled across the lawn, shielding her eyes from the sun while scanning the group for family. She greeted the hostess—her sister, Elena—and went over to sit with their mother, Helen.

Helen gave Scarlett a cheek kiss. "Would you like to borrow my cardigan?" she asked.

Scarlett had done a lot of cutting when she was in college. Her arms were covered by a network of raised scars. With the help of therapy, she found other ways to take care of her emotions and sensitivities. Wearing short sleeves was new for Scarlett, and she was still trying to set herself at ease with the feeling of being exposed.

"No, Mother," she answered. "Thank you, it's awfully hot, and I decided to dress for the weather. I'll be just fine."

Helen stiffened and wrinkled her brow. She narrowed her eyes at Scarlett. "This is Karly's event. You don't want to take the focus off her on this special day, do you? This isn't the way to get attention, Scarlett. Especially today when there are children everywhere, for goodness' sake."

"Would you like me to sit with someone else?" Scarlett asked. "Am I making you uncomfortable?"

Her mother responded, "What am I supposed to tell people? Surely you realize they can't help but notice. It might show up in photos, for that matter." She rolled her eyes. "Honestly, Scarlett, why do you always insist on being so indiscreet?"

Scenario Analysis

Families who have healthy relationships are capable of "differentiation," a term in psychology for maintaining close, caring relationships while recognizing family members as individuals who are different from one another. Helen was having a hard time with Scarlett's choice to allow her scars to be exposed because Helen felt others would judge her for her association with her daughter. Her discomfort came from anxiety that she would be viewed as a bad person or faulted for family members' problems.

Similarly, her other daughter, who was more conventional, served as an emotional prop for Helen; as long as Elena could serve as evidence of her good parenting, Helen could feel better about herself. Wanting to be perceived positively is normal and understandable—we all experience this desire—but keeping those feelings in check is healthy.

Parent Viewpoint

Helen was mystified by Scarlett. Why would she want to show herself off this way? And, of all places, at Elena's gracious home? It seemed like a deliberate provocation to shock her sister's guests. And given the occasion, it was unusually inconsiderate to show up in that state when she could have covered herself decently and not made people uncomfortable.

Did Scarlett expect people just to avert their eyes and not say anything? She looked like a victim of some terrible accident, or a house fire, perhaps. Her appearance certainly wasn't going to lead to any pleasant party chat. It was going to be a long afternoon.

Adult Child Viewpoint

Scarlett was working at feeling comfortable in her skin, scarred though it may be, and presenting herself as someone with visible problems who was nevertheless intact and confident. She had ended therapy long ago but knew this situation was another level of challenge and self-acceptance she needed to continue practicing.

Scarlett had more ability to differentiate than Helen; she could see her mother had many positive qualities although she sometimes said harsh, even cruel, things. She knew Helen felt distressed by seeing her scarred arms, but, nevertheless, Scarlett consciously tried to maintain her composure and not let her mother's emotions interfere with celebrating her niece's graduation.

Strategy Breakdown

Parents and children are not always a perfect fit in temperament. Genetics determine hair color, height, and facial features, but they also give us some measure of our personality. Sometimes family members have to extend themselves and make a significant effort to try to understand one another. Parents in this position can increase their empathy by recalling observations of their child as a small, helpless creature. You can reflect on differences among members of your family of origin and call to mind anything you appreciated or valued about people not like you. Sometimes it helps to look for qualities you admire in your child as they are now as an adult.

Helen couldn't relate to Scarlett as easily as she could to Elena, even when they were children. What she thought of as Scarlett's "awkward times" as a young adult left her feeling at a complete loss. Helen struggled with stepping outside her own viewpoint and empathizing because she focused on outward appearances.

Here are some communication strategies that could help Helen develop a better relationship with her adult child:

Show interest and curiosity. The respectful communication we first discussed in chapter 2 (see page 13) includes signaling that you want to hear the other person's point of view. In an ideal world, when Scarlett reached adulthood, Helen could use candor to bridge the gap between them. She might admit their different dispositions, saying, "You know, you were quite a serious child. I'm not at all surprised you chose a life of studying. I never really could tell what you were thinking, but you were very observant." Or she might explore Scarlett's point of view, asking, "What is your impression of these young women at this graduation? Do you think any of them will go in the direction you have? I sometimes wonder what it takes to devote yourself to learning in the way you've done."

Make repairs. Even if she's not ready to let go of her judgment, Helen can make an apologetic remark as a start toward better relations: "We're not as close as I'd like us to be, and I know some of it is me. Is there anything I can do to make things easier between us?" or "I know I can get a bit prickly. It's always okay to let me know when I'm out of bounds."

Adjust tone and body language. Helen tended to use a commanding, stern manner and could be intimidating. Softening her voice with Scarlett and using an inviting, open body posture would signal to Scarlett that she genuinely wanted to connect with her daughter.

Potential Pitfalls

To become themselves, your children must separate from you, whether it's getting wild haircuts or making impractical career decisions. Let them stand on their own. Try to overlook the parts that cause shock or disapproval and work to avoid these approaches:

Living in the past. Nostalgia is one thing but trying to relate to a younger version of your child rarely goes well. Parents and adult children who want to maintain a close connection must keep adjusting to one another's changes; as life progresses, they rediscover each other, over and over.

Dwelling on failures. Attempts to reconnect don't always succeed, but that doesn't mean you should give up. As the parent of an adult, you can continue finding new shared interests, new activities to bond over, and new levels of intimacy in conversation.

Tips to Remember

» **You're not in charge.** Pay attention to your wish to control your adult child or make them representatives of you. Consider that they are a separate being with a distinct personality and tastes.

» **Your memories have value.** Offer kind, yet candid, feedback on your observations and memories of your children—you can recall plenty they don't remember. Younger adults may enjoy reflecting with you on early signs of their current temperament or preferences. These were the sprouting clues to who they would eventually become.

» **You have wisdom to share.** If your adult child has kids of their own, encourage them to notice and cultivate the differences between their children. Siblings should have the option to play different sports or learn different musical instruments. This practice is not always convenient for the parents, but it allows the offspring to cultivate their independence.

Steps toward Reconnection

When parents feel distanced from their adult child's tastes, attire, or choice of partner, it helps to take a step back and practice accepting them as they are. Life is short, and we only have so much time to enjoy our children's company. Even if grown kids are doing something that doesn't seem true to who they are, young adulthood can be a time of exploration. Chances are they will move on to other things before long, especially if we let it go unremarked. Loving your child means maintaining that stance even when they seem unlovable. Doing so is part of what you signed up for.

Reflection Questions

» When did you test your parents' capacity to accept you?

» Do you ever notice yourself wishing your children looked better or achieved more? Maybe this notion comes up as hoping they will lose weight, dress or groom themselves differently, or advance in a career. What is it like to imagine letting go of those standards? What's the worst that could happen if you did?

» How are your hopes for your child's future related to your own wishes or regrets?

PART THREE

Relationship Issues with Your Adult Child

Each chapter in this section of the book offers two scenarios that focus on common relationship struggles that come up for parents and adult children. We'll review stories that focus on different issues and see how families can work through their problems as well as the mistakes that get made long the way. You'll learn how to handle similar situations in your own life, by employing healthy communication strategies to connect with your adult child.

Chapter 8

Divorce and Blended Families

People aged 50 and older are ending their marriages more often these days than they used to, which means the effects of divorce on adult children are more widespread. Even adults approaching midlife will experience an emotional reaction to their parents' separation or divorce. When parents get divorced late in life, their children often look back on their family histories and wonder if they missed something. Was their parents' marriage some sort of charade? They may feel some guilt if it becomes apparent their parents only stayed together for their sake. Children who grew up in unhappy families may ask what took their parents so long. Divorce or separation may splinter families, leading to increased isolation, but subsequent or reestablished relationships hold the possibility of reconfiguring and broadening support networks.

Bother of the Bride

Emma's parents, Alec and Lola, got divorced while she was in college. Alec remarried within the year and Lola found a new husband a couple of years after. Now it was Emma's turn to go to the altar with her fiancé, Shane. Shane's dad was no longer alive; his mother lived a thousand miles away but was enthusiastic and involved. However, Emma's side of the wedding party was complicated by her two sets of parents. As the wedding planning progressed, both Emma's parents put her in the middle of their disagreements, and each complained to her about the other.

Financing quickly became a bone of contention. Emma decided to invite her mother to lunch and try to get her to land an agreement with her father and leave Emma out if it.

Lola gave her a big hug and smooches at the restaurant, saying, "I'm so proud of you! I can't wait for your big day!" After they chatted a bit over cocktails, Emma got to the point, saying, "You know, Mom, I'd feel a lot more excited if you and Dad would sort out the money part of things. It's no fun being in the middle of this." She felt her irritation rise to the surface and kept going. "It's not fair you're both acting so childish. Instead of working things out you're each being selfish and stressing me out!"

Lola felt like she'd been slapped across the face. Here she thought they would have a nice celebratory lunch, but instead Emma was making a scene.

Scenario Analysis

Weddings are laden with symbolism and expectation, and planning them can be an extensive and draining process, as well as a substantial expense. When the parents are no longer married, complicated feelings and entrenched communication issues can raise the pressure to the boiling point. Lola and Alec genuinely wanted their daughter's day to be special, but they'd fallen back into their dynamic of using Emma's happiness as a pretext to express resentment and hostility to each other.

Parent Viewpoint

Lola was fed up with Alec and his slippery ways. She was doing everything she could think of to offer Emma a spectacular wedding—the one she had always dreamed of for her daughter. He needed to step up and chip in his fair share. It wasn't so much the money that irked her—Lola could fund the event by herself if it came to it—it was Alec trying to evade his responsibility as usual. He was the father of the bride and should act like it and not argue over every nickel and dime.

Adult Child Viewpoint

Emma remained genuinely confused about what had led to her parents' divorce. As she grew older, she concluded it may have just been an accumulation of little things that got to them both over time. She had never complained about their split or let her parents know how upset she really was about it. But seeing them act this way was bringing back all the sadness and confusion she'd felt during the messy, drawn-out divorce proceedings. Why couldn't her family get along the way other families did?

Strategy Breakdown

Parents whose relationship with each other undergoes a drastic change like divorce can, by the time the dust settles, lose sight of what's important to them—including their connection to their adult child. When negative feelings affect the way you communicate with your young adult, try reconnecting with your goals. What do you imagine when you picture the kind of relationship you want with your child? Chances are that using your child as a conduit for transmitting bad feelings to your ex is not what comes to mind.

Lola and Alec, caught up in the fighting they knew so well, got distracted from preserving their relationship to Emma. When Emma confronted Lola about this situation, Lola almost started crying. Emma's words were painful, but true. To salvage the conversation and move things in a positive direction, Lola relied on these strategies:

Engage in emotional reflection. Lola wanted Emma to know she understood what her daughter was saying. "Your father and I are bickering, and putting you in the middle of it. It's ruining what should be a happy experience for you. I'm sorry, sweetie."

Set boundaries. "The last thing I want is to let you down," she continued. "From now on, your father and I will figure this out between us. I will call him tonight and tell him we just have to come to terms, without dragging you into our drama."

Converse as equals. Lola's sincere apology and acceptance of responsibility shifted the dynamic. And she went further to show Emma that she respected her as an adult. Lola offered, "Can I tell you some things I'm having a hard time with, too? They're not about you," she hurried to add. Emma looked concerned. "Sure, what is it, Mom?"

"Well," Lola confessed. "I don't feel that comfortable being in the ceremony as a divorcée. It feels awkward, your father and I both being there with other partners."

"Mom, that's just crazy," Emma said. "Nobody thinks about it like that. Mario's the best. You two are so happy! And I'm glad."

Lola felt her eyes well up. "It's true, your dad and I . . . well, we weren't really right for each other . . . Oh, you've got me all emotional. I knew I'd cry at the wedding but this is ridiculous. We're supposed to be having lunch!"

Potential Pitfalls

Stay alert for these bad habits, which can be triggered by a tense relationship with a former spouse:

Creating unrealistic expectations. Even if you've put the past behind you, you may feel negative emotions when interacting with your ex. Be prepared to break away before things get heated. Emma's dad, Alec, had a way of bringing out Lola's temper. Emotions were heightened while planning this major life event, which along with Lola's own uncomfortable feelings about her divorce, made the situation hard for her to handle.

Misdirecting anger. As much as humanly possible, a parent's job is to do their best to manage their emotions and be a resource to their child. Be sure your issues with your spouse don't get projected onto other people.

Tips to Remember

» **Remember that disharmony is hard to see.** When your adult child is acting out of character while you're in conflict with your partner or spouse, the reason may be that the clash is painful for them to witness. Rely on your empathy to help you look for any underlying causes of their distress.

» **Keep communicating.** If you don't know how the conflict is affecting your child, venture a guess. If you're off base, they will tell you and probably clarify what's bothering them.

» **Admit you're imperfect.** When in doubt about how to discuss this kind of conflict with your adult child, try saying something vulnerable about what you're going through. You may be surprised at how readily they reconnect with you when you give them a chance to offer their support. Try phrases like "This is a hard conversation to have" or "I wish we could talk without arguing like this."

Steps toward Reconnection

When you've had an unpleasant exchange with your child, you can rely on these concepts to see you through:

Best intentions are most likely at play. Unless you have an unusually troubled history as a family, chances are you fundamentally like and accept each other. You both want to find happiness and share some goodwill. When the going gets tough, hold on to that.

Your strong rapport is a powerful source of reconnection. The bond between you and your child is likely to endure for your entire lifetime. Families can sustain hard knocks and come out on the other side. When all else fails, the rapport you developed through teaching them to tie their shoes or baking a cake will always be between you. You might need to step away from fights or take time to see each other's point of view, but, eventually, you will both find your way to reconnecting.

Better to be happy than right. Try to let things go, and let your child be a separate person. Don't hold on to any disagreement to the bitter end.

Change of Plans

Deb came out later in life. She and her husband reached an amicable divorce after she came to understand she was a lesbian. They shared custody of their two middle school–aged daughters, Charlotte and Sylvia. Deb's family of origin had been distant for many years and became entirely estranged when she let them know of her life changes.

Deb wanted to do all she could to help the girls keep in touch with their grandparents on their dad's side of the family, Lin and Blanche. The grandparents lived a couple of hours away and their tradition was to take the girls along to their timeshare at the start of summer break, where they enjoyed a variety of kid-oriented activities and a colossal swimming pool.

This year Deb decided to sign up for the Pride parade float sponsored by her employer. She was excited about attending a large gay community event for the first time. The girls overheard her sharing her plans with a friend and insisted they go, too. As luck would have it, Pride day conflicted with the dates they were supposed to see Blanche and Lin.

Deb braced herself and picked up the phone. She ended up leaving a voice mail but heard back from Blanche the next day, who explained, "You know we accept you, and we love you, Deb. We're just concerned about your new lifestyle and the effect it might have on the girls. We want them to grow up normal and have the same social opportunities as other kids. Do they even allow children at that parade?"

Deb took a breath. "Why yes, Blanche, the thing is, they want to go because their friends are part of the show."

"Well," said Blanche, "what about letting us have them like we planned this summer and later we can talk about next year? They'll be older then."

"I know, Blanche; I think that's actually part of the problem. They're old enough now and they want to be with their friends. You know how it is for teenagers. It's really important to us they get to see you and Lin this summer, but I'm afraid we're going to need to pick some different dates. I'm really sorry." Blanche sighed, "All right, then. I guess I should let you get off the phone, Deb. I'm going to need to talk to Lin. Give our love to the girls."

Scenario Analysis

When couples divorce, the former spouse may often have to communicate with their former in-laws about grandchildren. It's important that both sides maintain civil discourse. Deb knew Blanche would not like changing their plans but hadn't anticipated the larger questions that would arise once she asked to reschedule. She wasn't prepared for Blanche challenging her sexuality or worrying that the parade would somehow harm the girls. Blanche, on the other hand, was disappointed that her grandchildren didn't want to come out. For her and Lin, those weeks together were always the highlight of the year. Her goal was to preserve the relationship so she steered the conversation back to practical matters and was able to maintain her focus. Deb also knew Blanche well enough to believe she was not a malicious person and was probably reacting out of her anxiety about changes in the family.

Parent Viewpoint

Lin and Blanche had anticipated their usual summer plans would go as expected. After the divorce, they thought it was all the more important to maintain a family tradition to assure the girls that their life hadn't been completely upended. They were disappointed because the timeshare vacation wouldn't be the same without the kids along to liven things up.

Blanche felt like Deb had gotten a little withdrawn when she had raised questions about the girls' reaction to having a gay parent. But Blanche was their grandma; she had a right to know about these things. What if their friends made fun of them or got mean?

Adult Child Viewpoint

Deb was startled at Blanche's remarks. She had known her message to change plans would come as a surprise to the grandparents, but she wasn't prepared for the negative comments about the effect of her lesbian identity on the kids. Still, she reasoned, better to know what they think so we can talk about it. She thought about what she could say to Blanche and Lin; Blanche clearly had some misconceptions going on. She seemed to think the kids needed to be protected from Deb's identity, when they had no trouble embracing it and had already learned to handle unkind comments from peers.

Strategy Breakdown

After divorce, grandparents often wonder what their role will be, and in-laws may feel especially uncertain about the frequency of contact they can expect and how much control they will have in seeing their grandkids. These concerns can come to the surface when there's a disagreement.

Blanche recounted her conversation to Lin. He replied, "Well, we knew they were going to outgrow us one of these days, didn't we?"

Blanche had worries beyond the change in plans. "But do you think it's good for them to go to that parade?" she asked Lin. "Who's going to watch them if Deb's with her friends from work? What if something happens? They can't just go off by themselves; they're just kids."

Blanche fretted about their conversation for a few days and decided to call her former daughter-in-law back. But this time Blanche used a few methods from chapter 2 to keep the conversation open and honest (see page 13).

Take a respectful tone. Blanche used the time to collect her thoughts. She decided her strategy would be to let Deb know about her worries without calling Deb's parenting into question. She would trust they both had the best interests of the girls in mind. Blanche wanted to be calm and respectful.

Converse as an equal. Blanche had considered already what troubled her about this new situation and had a response ready. She spoke directly and honestly and didn't offer unsolicited advice. "I want to know how you're going to keep an eye on them in a parade if you're in it yourself. And how are you going to keep them safe?" Blanche sighed, "I admit, I'm sad they won't be visiting and it's probably making me anxious about the parade."

Deb was equally respectful in her answer. "You're right that keeping them safe, especially in a big crowd, is a priority," she said. "The girls will be with another parent. Please don't worry about that."

"Is there anything else bothering you?" Deb asked Blanche.

Offer more positive comments than negative. "I'm always struck by how well the girls have adjusted to the divorce," Blanche said. "They're so secure in how much you love them. And Lin and I are so grateful you include us in their lives." Then Blanche divulged her other concerns. "But I worry about them. Do the other kids at school know why their parents got divorced? Are the girls having any problems with other kids? When I was in school, kids people thought were gay usually got beat up pretty bad."

Deb realized that a lack of information was feeding Blanche's fears. She let Blanche know the girls were adjusting well, and they were getting a lot of support from friends and their families. Blanche felt at ease and was ready to talk about rescheduling.

Potential Pitfalls

When navigating communication issues within a blended family, check yourself for:

Overreacting. Reacting with intense emotions doesn't get good results. Blanche had used the time between calls to get over her initial upset and focused on specific concerns she could then address by talking to Deb.

Taking things personally. Initially it sounded to Deb like Blanche was unfairly challenging her parenting choices. That might have led to a fight and could have resulted in Deb refusing to continue the conversation. Deb, however, kept a cool head and initiated a follow-up conversation that allowed Blanche to explain the concerns that had been at the root of her questioning.

Tips to Remember

When overwhelmed with emotion in a tough interaction, remind yourself to take these steps:

» **Pause and reflect.** It's always better to stop a conversation than to allow it to become destructive. Just by buying yourself some time, you win. Take a breath.

» **Demonstrate respect.** Go back to the foundational skills from chapter 2 of affirming your connection and communicating as equals (see page 13). For Deb and Blanche, that meant taking each other's concerns seriously and putting in the time to share worries and consider options.

» **Attempt repairs.** If you're both distressed, this method may not work immediately, but using phrases like "Let's take a step back" or "I'm sorry, I shouldn't have put it that way. Can I try again?" interrupts escalating feelings and allows a reset of the conversation.

Steps toward Reconnection

In a blended family, chances are that common interests will pull people together after a disagreement. Deb and Blanche's advantage was their mutual interest in the girls, which united them toward a common purpose. Look for any shared interests and keep coming back to them when trying to repair a division. Put the focus on where your interests and concerns overlap, rather than on your differences, with language like "I know we both want the best for . . ." and "In the end, what matters is . . ."

Reflection Questions

» The families in this chapter ended up feeling closer because they had to handle a conflict together. Have you ever experienced this situation yourself or seen it happen in your family?

» How do you think conflicts can lead to increased intimacy in relationships?

» When is this potential present, and when does conflict trend in a harmful or destructive direction? What differentiates these situations?

Chapter 9

Your Grandchildren and You

Quarreling is common when parents and adult children disagree about how children are being raised. Parents of an adult child can feel disconnected and distant from their grandchildren, who are growing up in a very different world than they did.

In some cases, parents and their adult child clash over whether there will even be grandchildren in the family. According to *Time* magazine, 55 percent of today's younger Americans regard marrying or having children as "not very important." They value education and financial and career goals above those conventional milestones of adulthood. Cultural shifts like these contribute to tension between the generations. Nevertheless, today's younger adults often maintain emotional ties to their parents long beyond what used to be expected.

Nobody's Grandma

Barb and Dennis had always looked forward to becoming grandparents. But when the topic of children had come up during their last visit with their son and daughter-in-law, Ryan made it clear: He and Lindsey had firmly decided they would not have kids.

The conversation started because as they had cocktails, Ryan and Lindsey talked about travel and not wanting to buy a house yet. Since Dennis was in real estate, he wanted to help; he had connections. Ryan got a little agitated and told Dennis, "We already told you we're doing other things and aren't planning to settle down anytime soon." Lindsey added, "As a journalist, I have to be ready to pick up and move around on short notice."

Dennis was obviously put off and shook the ice in his drink.

Barb felt the need to smooth things over. "Well, honey, maybe you'll end up moving back here someday," she added. Instead of the intended effect, that comment turned out to be a conversation stopper, and she got no response. This silence caused Barb to natter on anxiously: "I mean, anything can happen, right? You could come back here and start your family. Who knew I'd get pregnant when your dad and I least expected it? Then the next thing we knew, there we were, the two of us practically kids ourselves, trying to figure out what to do next."

Ryan cut in. "Mom, we are surprisingly capable of planning our own future, and it doesn't involve children. You're going to have to let go of that fantasy."

Scenario Analysis

Barb wants to connect with Ryan and be a part of his adult life. Dennis tried to do the same by using his professional skills to offer assistance and support. What they don't realize is that

Ryan feels as though they don't accept him and are not curious about who he is now. It is as though he has been assigned the role of son but follows a different script from theirs. The parents in this case will need to take a step back and show their earnest wish to update themselves on Ryan's current aspirations and plans. They have their ideas of who he is, but they have not explored his world as an adult very deeply.

Parent Viewpoint

Barb knew they had said they didn't want children but expected they would change their minds. With this latest pronouncement, however, she realized she should have taken what they said originally more seriously. After the tiff, the young adults acted distant and went off by themselves for the rest of the weekend visit. Barb realized she was still feeling terribly sad about, well, everything. The botched visit, the idea of never being anybody's grandma, feeling like she barely even saw her son anymore. It was all too much.

Adult Child Viewpoint

Ryan made this visit to his parents knowing he and Lindsey might be doing some ambitious traveling for the foreseeable future. He wasn't sure when he would see them again and had hoped their time together would be enjoyable and relaxed. He didn't expect a deep connection or searching conversations, but he wanted to be on good terms with his folks. After the argument, he felt terrible about how terse he'd been. But it was usually so alienating to try to talk with his parents about anything personal or meaningful to him. They both always had a lot to say, but he had come to realize they were just not the best listeners.

Strategy Breakdown

Parents usually have strong opinions about their children's reproductive decisions. Many parents spend decades looking toward the future, imagining the gratification they will feel from being grandparents. Others think parenthood will make their child miserable and want to warn them away from having kids.

Barb and Dennis would have an uphill climb to sort out the situation with Ryan and Lindsey. Their son was disengaged and had little motivation to reconnect with them. Knowing he was planning extended travel gave them a nudge to try to mend the rift while they had a chance. They had been unaware of Ryan's difficult feelings toward them that he'd hinted at. His method of dealing with family issues was to make himself scarce and maintain only minimal communication.

Barb confided in a friend, who urged Barb to contact the friend's family therapist. With the therapist's advice, Barb decided to send an email to Ryan. She apologized for causing distress, using the following strategies of emotional reflection from chapter 2 (see page 14) to demonstrate that she could see why he felt or believed the way he did.

Offer a clear apology. "I'm sorry I brought up topics that were intrusive when you visited."

Accept responsibility. "I know I need to let you live your own life the way you want."

Name the offense. "You have every right to make your own choices; my job as a parent is to support you, not argue for what I want."

Acknowledge harm. "When I insert my opinions about your personal decisions, I can see how that's disrespectful to both you and your wife."

Outline a plan to move forward. "In the future, I will be asking questions and listening instead of trying to drive the conversation."

Barb learned in therapy that merely saying "I'm sorry" or "I'm sorry I hurt your feelings" is inadequate, especially in a strained relationship. A genuine apology gives evidence of soul searching and labor; that you've looked at things from the other person's perspective and see what you need to change and why.

Potential Pitfalls

Whether it's an issue relating to grandchildren or something else, avoid these bad habits, which escalate conflicts:

Mixing alcohol with sensitive discussions. Although it's ordinary for people to drink at social gatherings, anything more than one drink during a touchy conversation could lead to impulsive or regrettable remarks.

Putting your pride first. Parents who feel it's beneath them to apologize to their adult child should reexamine their family's power structure. What are you losing by conceding an error or oversight? Admitting your flawed nature gives your child the grace to forgive and accept you as one adult to another.

Tips to Remember

Barb and Dennis want to learn more about Ryan's life now, so they can get reacquainted by:

» **Asking thoughtful questions.** Genuine curiosity shows the other person you care about the subject at hand and are sincerely open to whatever they have to say.

» **Engaging attentive listening.** It's possible to interject gestures, like nodding and appreciative sounds—"Interesting," "Okay," or "I didn't know that"—to encourage a speaker to keep talking without interrupting them.

» **Validating.** Signaling agreement to the speaker's points—"You're right" or "What you said makes sense"—signals that we understand them and can see why they feel or believe the way they do.

Steps toward Reconnection

The power of storytelling can be a helpful tool for repairing rifts if discussing a difficult matter. Parents can share family history, telling stories of relatives with similar attitudes or experiences to the current situation. The older person can help the younger one see that each experience in life adds to the next.

Barb tried this tactic but it backfired because it was about having a baby, which her son doesn't want to experience. Next time she shared a story about traveling with Dennis on their honeymoon to make a connection with her son and daughter-in-law.

The Daisy Factor

Ray and Alicia provided childcare every day to their two grandchildren, ages two and four, because their son Eddie's wife had died of cancer a few months ago. The family was settling in to a new normal after the ordeal of Connie's illness and death, but everything still felt raw for all of them.

Eddie would drop the kids off when he went to work in the morning, or sometimes Ray would hop over and get them if things were running late. Caring for two young children was exhausting, but the grandparents were glad to do it for as long as Eddie needed to give everybody time to adjust.

The struggle they were having, though, was with Eddie's dog, Daisy, a rescue Eddie and Connie had adopted before the kids came along. Eddie didn't want to put her in dog day-care due to the expense. So Daisy came along with the kids to Ray and Alicia's house. She was affectionate but would chew things, snatch food, and bark and get excited when the kids made noise. Ray and Alicia's nerves were getting frayed.

When Eddie came to get the kids one evening, Ray asked him, "Hey, when is a good time to chat? I wanted to run a couple of things by you." Eddie was distracted with the children and suggested his dad call after bedtime. When Ray reached him on the phone, Eddie was yawning and had just gotten Eli to bed. "What's on your mind, Dad?"

"Eddie, your mom and I love having the kids as much as we can, but with Daisy in the mix, it's a bit much. She's sure a sweet dog but—"

Eddie interrupted him: "Dad, she's part of the family. I can't just dump her someplace. What do you expect me to do?"

Scenario Analysis

People have varying levels of attachment and commitment to their pets. This topic often represents one of those differences in values that can be deeply emotional and difficult to discuss. In this case, Eddie had been devastated by the loss of his wife, and Daisy was one of the links he still had to her, which added intensity to his reaction.

As soon as he started the conversation, Ray knew he had caught Eddie at a lousy time. And yet there seemed to be no right time for this upsetting discussion.

Parent Viewpoint

Ray knew he hit a nerve. The dog was too much and his son was still reeling from his wife's death. He tried to figure out how to backpedal after Eddie's reaction. "I can tell I upset you. Your mom and I want to do everything we possibly can for you and the kids, really we do. Nothing against Daisy. We can leave this and talk about it later. Get some rest. Goodnight."

Adult Child Viewpoint

Eddie was ready to burst into tears. Did his dad really want him to give up Daisy? How much more loss did he have to take? He was so boxed in being a single parent; his life felt unmanageable. The idea of having to make any new arrangements seemed like the last straw. And the kids needed Daisy for security. They loved her, and causing more upheaval in their lives wouldn't be fair to them.

Strategy Breakdown

When parents have to help an overburdened adult child manage the practical and emotional aftermath of a tragedy, things go much better with good conflict management skills. Despite everyone's love and support for one another, there are bound to be times when the pressures and challenges of life lead to a heated exchange.

In this case, Ray skillfully calmed Eddie after bringing up Daisy's behavior issues. He de-escalated Eddie's distress and smoothed things over by acknowledging neither of them were in good enough shape to handle a tough conversation. Then he assured Eddie of his wish to help, concluded their exchange, and left an opening to follow up. Communication techniques like this one can act as a temporary fix until we are capable of a more meaningful discussion. Ray resolved to arrange a do-over and give the conversation another try. To do so, he turned to these strategies:

Affirm the mutual connection. Ray saw Eddie at drop-off the next morning and wished him a good day, reestablishing their connection and showing he wanted to be on good terms. When Eddie came to pick the kids up that evening, the kids were with Alicia in the front room watching a video. Ray invited Eddie to join him in the kitchen.

Signal respect. "Sorry for the bad timing last night, buddy," Ray said to his son. "I won't keep you. I know you probably want to get everybody bundled off home. I just wanted to see if you can give me any tips on how we can help get Daisy to calm down, since it sounds like she's going to be coming around for a while." Ray made it clear he was respecting Eddie's resistance to changing their arrangement with Daisy.

Converse rather than lecture. Ray might have presented a long list of the furniture, pillows, and other items Daisy had left her toothmarks on. Instead of ranting about his grievances, he took the attitude that this problem was for the two of them to solve. "If we could just get her to stop chewing on things she's not supposed to," he continued, "that would be a big help."

Eddie responded in kind, saying, "Dad, I don't know what to tell you. It's all about the relationship. I'm not going to lie; she's not all that calm at home with me, either. I just love her so much, I put up with it. I know she gets into everything."

Find common ground. After some further discussion, they hit on the idea of finding a trainer or some other resource who would help them change Daisy's bad habits. Eddie agreed to reach out to the rescue organization that had fostered Daisy to see if they could provide some leads.

Potential Pitfalls

Ray hadn't always been able to handle conflict with his son this well. He and Ray struggled in the past with these common behaviors, which are ones to try to steer clear of:

Creating power struggles. Whenever Ray tried to impose his will and authority on Eddie, Eddie would reflexively rebel against him. Ray learned to talk things through with Eddie and explain the reason behind his point of view, often finding that his son would accept a well-reasoned argument.

Maintaining inflexibility. Ray had been raised to believe that once a son was an adult, he shouldn't need any help from his parents. But seeing Eddie's plight, and the pain he was going through, opened Ray's eyes. He could see Eddie was already stretched to the breaking point and couldn't manage another challenge.

Having unrealistic expectations. Early on, Ray had been critical of Eddie's ways of parenting his children. But he began to see his son as another adult trying his best to raise his kids, just as Ray once had been.

Tips to Remember

The next time you face an unavoidable conflict in your family, try these ideas:

» **Arrange optimal conditions.** Seek out the best place for a difficult discussion. A quiet location where you can concentrate and feel comfortable allows everyone to bring their best selves.

» **Affirm you're playing on the same team.** Begin with comments that reflect your positive attitude.

» **Agree on clear expectations.** Maybe you won't arrive at a perfect solution in one conversation; plan a follow-up discussion so everyone can approach the situation fresh.

Steps toward Reconnection

Ray had come on a bit strong with Eddie on the phone call and hadn't thought about the state his son might be in by the end of the day. It's possible to stop a conversation that's going in a bad direction and salvage the moment before too much damage is done. When you sense a negative shift in a discussion, adopt the habit of commenting on what's going on to check if you are "reading the room" correctly. Language to try includes:

"It sounds like now is not the best time."

"This doesn't seem to be going too well. Shall I try again?"

"Would it be better if we talk later? You sound like you might be distracted."

"Wait a second, did I go too far? I don't want to offend you."

"If I'm being too pushy, please let me know. It's just that I'm concerned about you."

Reflection Questions

» Grandparents are said to enjoy the best of both worlds, having children in their lives but not being entirely responsible for their care. If you are a grandparent, is it everything you expected? If you're not a grandparent yet, what do you savor when you anticipate having grandchildren?

» How do you think you would respond if your child announced, like Ryan and Lindsey, that they did not intend to have children?

» What memories do you recall of your grandparents? Did they, or do they now, seem to have gained any wisdom or insight they have communicated to you?

Chapter 10

Traditions, Birthdays, and Holidays

Traditions, birthdays, and holidays connect us to our cultural group by providing a shared experience. All three involve continuity and repetition. We can rely on these markers as the year progresses or as we move through a lifetime as a family.

Children learn who they belong to and where they come from through family traditions, during holidays or otherwise. These events represent our history and values, so beyond the stories they hear, children share experiences showing them what matters to their family. Traditions help them connect to their kin, and give them a feeling of predictability and repetition that is comforting. Get-togethers and special occasions can also be stressful, though, because relatives have different needs or expectations.

Crisis Averted

The Marshalls had a big family reunion every three years, and all involved made special efforts to arrange travel and time off from work to attend the gathering. The siblings and cousins had grown and were married; by now, the event required renting several adjoining vacation homes, involving considerable planning and logistics, but it was a beloved occasion.

One person who was not having a good time, though, was Elijah. He had been four years old at the last reunion; this time, he was almost eight. One evening the cousins in his age group were occupied with board games, but he was weeping tears of frustration. His mom, Nina, was embarrassed and not sure how to handle all the noise he was making. Elijah was a shy kid, and she knew a crowd this size would be a lot for him, but she hadn't expected him to get this upset.

His grandfather, Nina's father-in-law, was on his way back from the kitchen with a beer when he noticed his grandson's distress. "Hey little man, what's going on?" he asked. Eli kept sobbing and was having trouble catching his breath, rocking back and forth while he wrapped his arms tightly around his body. Nina answered, "Oh Pop, I don't know. Something happened with the other kids—he said they're not playing by the rules and now he's a mess. He's got me worn out. I'd like a drink myself."

Pop knelt by Eli and gently put his hands on his shoulders. "Go get off your feet, honey," he told Nina. "I've helped his daddy through so many of these little fits when he was this tall. We can work it out. Right, young fella?"

As Nina sat down, several women started asking her questions. "Is he always like that?" "What's the matter with your boy?" "Is he alright? 'Cause my kids do not need to see that type of tantrum."

She was holding back tears, and even though family surrounded her, Nina felt terribly alone. Elijah was overwhelmed by too many strangers, with too much noise and unfamiliar surroundings. Nina knew because it was happening to her, too.

Scenario Analysis

It is natural to imagine being surrounded by our family as a cause for joy, but feeling stressed in that situation, especially on special occasions, is expected. Eli was overstimulated and didn't have his usual routine and familiar toys, comfort objects he relied on to calm himself. His mother, Nina, was feeling drained from being responsible for him while her husband socialized with his siblings.

Grandfather "Pop" had seen other children in the state Eli was experiencing and knew they needed one-on-one, calming attention from an adult. He could see Nina was frazzled and unable to give Eli what he needed. So he stepped in to help his grandson with a calming distraction.

Parent Viewpoint

Pop saw the boy crying and getting upset and knew Elijah needed to be some adult's top priority. He was glad to help, remembering a couple of his sons being sensitive like that when they were small.

He wondered where Andre was, and thought he should look for him to let him know his family probably needed more help. He helped Eli get busy, gave him the job of loading the dishwasher with him, and told him some stories about his dad when his dad was small while they worked. Pretty soon Eli was ready to go with Pop to see what the kids were up to and to try to find a different game he could join.

Adult Child Viewpoint

Nina felt inadequate and overwhelmed. She had enjoyed the previous reunion because Eli was smaller and mostly clung to her side, so she could visit with other adults and not worry too much about how he was doing. She knew why he was upset, but it was difficult to find a quiet place to soothe him in this environment. And she had to admit, she wanted time to socialize and didn't want to miss out on any fun. Doing round-the-clock childcare with her stressed-out boy for several days was not her idea of a vacation.

Now she felt alienated and excluded. It seemed like she and Eli were bothering everybody just by being there. Didn't other people's kids ever fall apart? What was the big deal?

Strategy Breakdown

Children get overloaded in situations they're not used to. And with any large family group, this kind of scene is going to happen eventually. You see your grown child, or an in-law, struggling with their distressed offspring and it's an awkward situation. You want to help, but how to do so tactfully?

Most people are reluctant to accept feedback on their parenting; even at a calm time, many of us quickly become defensive on this topic, so it's a real challenge to get involved when everybody is already upset. Even when it seems obvious the parent badly needs help, tact is everything. Avoid a hurried or authoritarian tone, and make sure you are calm and patient. Use body posture and a soothing voice to show your wish to support, not criticize. (Note that these strategies are intended for close family members—not a stranger whose child is having a meltdown in the grocery store.)

Pop had good instincts.

Connect with the parent before attending to the child. Try an address like, "Can I help at all?" or "Are you two doing okay?"

Get verbal or nonverbal permission. If the adult looks relieved you asked or starts talking openly to you, that's enough of a green light.

Offer support. You can ask the adult, "Would you like a minute to catch your breath?" or "Is it okay if I try something?"

Switch gears. Once the adult seems comfortable, give the upset child your focused attention. Size up whether they will respond to physical comfort or if they need space. Talk calmly, and direct your voice at them only, not their parent. The words you say matter less than using your voice to set the tempo and volume you want them to match.

Be friendly. Use the child's name as you try to connect with them. Pop used affectionate terms, but if you are not already in the habit of using those with the child, just use their first name.

Few families have the benefit of living in proximity to one another where the generations can mix regularly and offer mutual support. Don't let that stop you from extending help, though. Parents of young children are often too physically and emotionally exhausted to be effective with their children every waking hour and are likely to appreciate even a brief respite when offered skillfully from a parent or family member.

Potential Pitfalls

The flip side of a close family is that everyone feels comfortable providing their two cents, especially when it comes to raising children.

Piling on. Nina's female relatives may have been trying to provide support and connect with her, but their words were overwhelming to her. Because they were all talking at once, their comments and questions felt like belittling criticisms to Nina.

Being a bystander. If you spot a parent or your grown child looking or sounding upset, don't add to the chorus. Instead, offer some privacy so they can keep their dignity if they get emotionally overwhelmed.

Tips to Remember

» **Family togetherness requires accommodations.** Being sensitive to everyone's needs will ensure gatherings are enjoyable for all participants. Some people, like Eli, are stressed by the change in routine, so making private or quieter spaces available is a good idea.

» **Be the one who helps.** Using good manners and your powers of observation, try offering your assistance to younger people who aren't comfortable at a gathering. Doing so is your rightful role and is worth the effort, so if you have something to give, don't hold back.

Steps toward Reconnection

Follow-up is important to make sure a stressful incident feels resolved. Pop could bring Eli back to Nina once Eli feels better so they can both see how she is doing. He could acknowledge her sharing her son by saying something like, "Thanks for letting me borrow him. It turns out he's got a knack for helping." Doing so shows respect for her status as Eli's parent. He could also seek out his son, Andre, for a quiet conversation later to share observations about Eli. This way, he could offer Andre insights about what Andre was like as a child and tell him how he helped Eli through tough times.

Charisse's Castle

Charisse was having a birthday. Her grandparents were coming over to see her open her presents and share a cake with seven candles. Her mother, Evelyn, had gotten a few simple gifts with trendy wrapping paper, but she was trying to keep clutter down. She and Charisse's dad both worked full-time and they got tired of toys underfoot. Evelyn saw her mom, Colleen, come in with her dad carrying a bulky gift as Charisse ran to greet them. "Grandpa and I are excited to see how you like your present, Birthday Girl!" called Colleen.

Charisse ran off to her room while the adults got settled.

"What on earth is that?" Evelyn nearly hissed at her mother. Colleen made a shushing motion, saying, "Don't worry. It's going to be a big hit!"

They all had some cake together and then it was time for the big moment. The grandparents helped Charisse open her gift: a brightly colored five-foot-tall pink princess tent to put up in her bedroom. Colleen explained she and Charisse had seen it on a TV ad, and when she saw Charisse's reaction, she couldn't resist buying it. "Charisse can tuck her toys inside and have her own little hideaway!"

Then Colleen noticed Evelyn's expression and added quietly, "I know it isn't what you would have chosen. I thought if it were in her bedroom, it wouldn't bother you. She was so excited about it."

Evelyn sighed, "If you had just asked, Mom. Now I'm going to have to look at it every day. You know I don't want her to get programmed to feel like she's supposed to have a bunch of girly type stuff. It's so harmful for girls to get caught up in the whole pink-princess-and-Barbie thing. You know where I stand on that."

Scenario Analysis

The princess tent was just a gift, but it wasn't simple at all. In choosing this present, Colleen was trying to give Charisse a specific kind of childhood experience. She felt her daughter, Evelyn, was depriving her granddaughter of feeling light-hearted, silly, and joyful, and she wanted to make up for it. Meanwhile, Evelyn had her own agenda for her young daughter; she wanted Charisse to feel strong and capable, not like a princess who needed to be rescued by somebody else. Evelyn also required order and simplicity in the household. She wanted a minimalist home because, as a working parent, she had "maximalist" responsibilities.

Parent Viewpoint

Colleen had seen Charisse's thrill at the ad for the princess tent and had felt compelled to get it because of her obvious joy over the thing. When she heard the poor child had gotten a coat for a birthday present, she felt pleased with herself for the decision. What little girl is going to get any delight out of a new coat? It sounded like something out of the Depression, for goodness' sake.

Her daughter was a bit sober and practical, and Colleen often felt like it was up to her to bring the frivolity and playfulness out in Charisse. After all, what was childhood for? There was time enough to be tidy and organized later in life. Colleen liked a bit of chaos and felt it was important for kids to enjoy creative freedom. She hadn't repressed Evelyn, who was a charming and bouncy little girl, and she was puzzled at why her daughter seemed to have such a need for control these days.

Adult Child Viewpoint

Evelyn thought the tent was dreadful. In terms of gender stereotyping, it wasn't the message she wanted to give her daughter. She couldn't imagine where her mother had gotten the idea that she should drag this thing into her home.

Charisse was delighted to show off her gift; she was happily going in and out, carrying her toys inside. Maybe this tent would make it easier to get her to pick up her things? Still, the fact that Colleen had shown up with this gift, unannounced, was inconsiderate. She felt like her mother had no respect for her parenting decisions.

Evelyn took a deep breath and decided she would do her best to compromise. If Charisse loved this thing, she would try to find a way to live with it. And she could see her mother knew she had crossed a line.

Strategy Breakdown

Parents are used to their position of greater power in relation to their children. Many have never gotten into the habit of admitting to their child when they've caused problems. Demonstrating respect is key when you're making this adjustment, and an attitude of respect makes it easier to humble yourself and admit being fallible after an error.

An apology is a powerful form of conflict management (see page 18). Here are pointers:

Reduce distractions. Colleen made sure to seek Evelyn out for a private moment as they tidied up later that day. When it was just the two of them, they could concentrate on their conversation uninterrupted. Even if one of them cried or had a big reaction, there was nothing to be embarrassed about with nobody else around.

Admit fault. Colleen said to Evelyn, "I'm sorry for springing the surprise on you like this. It would have been better to talk to you first. I see that now." Without justifying herself or making excuses, Colleen took responsibility for hurting Evelyn's feelings.

Name what you did. Show you understand the error or misjudgment that took place. "I got carried away with trying to please Charisse, but I didn't think about the effect it would have on you," Colleen continued.

Commit to doing better. Colleen concluded, "You're the parent, and you are in charge here. Next time, I'm going to run ideas by you before I make decisions."

Evelyn felt relieved and much more gracious toward Colleen after their conversation. As they wiped the counters and finished up, they fantasized about Evelyn doing an all-pink makeover on the rest of the house to match the princess tent, and this idea got them laughing together.

Saying sorry isn't always easy, but doing so helps parents and their grown children get along and indicates the balance of power is between you as adults. Expanding on the apology, though, to show you have given thought to the problem and recognize your part in it, goes much further in tending to your adult child's emotions.

Potential Pitfalls

Grandparents must be diplomats if they want to stay connected to the entire family. They have a lot to keep track of! When someone becomes offended, be the first to offer a gracious attitude.

Missing the signs. Colleen was caught up in the surprise as the party started, but she knew Evelyn well enough to perceive her mood and responded to it. If she hadn't noticed how Evelyn became deflated at the start of the event, the incident would have mushroomed in Evelyn's mind.

Letting things fester. Evelyn already felt overlooked and could have interpreted Colleen as trying to take over the party or deliberately bringing a showy gift to win over Charisse. But Colleen knew it was always best to address problems sooner than later. When we start viewing a family member's actions as hostile, that version of events becomes quite convincing as time passes.

Tips to Remember

» **Change is inevitable.** The generations of a family must find ways to keep power evenly distributed so everyone has enough influence and control. Like finely tuned machinery, the way people make decisions and resolve troubles is lively and dynamic. The authority you had as the parent of a young child doesn't last forever.

» **Everyone contributes to harmony.** When each person manages their rights and responsibilities in the family, everybody experiences contentment and pride in belonging to a group where people can trust each other, and where they can expect to be treated kindly and fairly.

» **To err is human.** A healthy family makes allowances for mistakes. Everyone's flaws are accepted; people strive to understand one another. This situation makes people less likely to get defensive or isolate themselves when they make a misstep, because they can feel confident nobody expects them to be perfect. Knowing our relatives can live with, and even embrace, our faults helps the family feel emotionally safe and gives everyone a sanctuary from a harsh world.

Steps toward Reconnection

When the parent can own up to mistakes, they set a fine example for younger generations to follow. Being able to say when we are wrong helps others believe in us.

Conversely, trying to act like we're infallible makes people think we're dishonest, trying to keep up a perfect front. Integrity means being "whole," which includes our weak and less awesome parts. When children live with parents who insist they are always right, they are taught to cover up and lie about their mistakes. In families where blunders are put in perspective, younger people learn to value themselves and others, warts and all.

Reflection Questions

» Celebrations, holidays, and gatherings are wonderful times for families to feel connected and to affirm their identity as a special group. What experiences do you recall of conflict or tension, even when attending something that was supposed to be enjoyable?

» How do you prepare yourself or your family for upcoming events? You might talk about what to expect, remember past events and what was fun or not-very-fun about them, share wishes and hopes, or try out other strategies.

» When things have not gone according to plan, how do you calm yourself and those around you so moods stay on an even keel?

Chapter 11

Distance and Disconnect

Whether you want your child to resume a relationship that fell by the wayside or travel to visit you more often, the way you act toward them can offer assurance they will enjoy your time together. You may need to change the way you behave so you can help them feel at ease, such as by catching up with their current version of themselves and letting them make changes to their lives without any negative remarks. If there are emotional risks involved in getting reacquainted, your child will need you to show them the effort is worthwhile. There are also practical concerns. Adults who have to deal with the expense and inconvenience of pausing their responsibilities to be able to visit you will do so more readily if they know they will be welcomed and set at ease.

Building Trust

Erica was considering whether to reconnect with her parents after several years with no communication. She had cut herself off from her family when they didn't accept her gender transition as a woman. Recently she'd been communicating with them online in brief messages. They'd exchanged small talk so far about movies, food, and what other family members were up to. Today Erica felt ready to talk on a deeper level.

Her parents, Monica and Frank, had said they'd been meeting with a therapist to learn how they could support her. Erica had looked up the therapist online; the website seemed credible. Erica's parents lived two hours away, and she was open to planning a day trip in the near future.

Her parents appeared on the screen for a FaceTime chat, waving hello. After a few minutes, Erica asked, "What can you do to assure me I'll be comfortable if we have a visit in person? Do you two have any ideas on what the ground rules would be?"

Frank responded quickly, "We're going to use your pronouns. We've been practicing with our therapist. And there won't be any deadnaming." Frank's use of the term demonstrated his awareness of the distress that calling Erica by her birth name instead of her chosen name would cause.

Monica joined in. "We want to let you set the pace. We can talk about what you want to talk about. And if you say something is off-limits, we'll change the subject."

Monica continued, chattering a bit nervously. "My friend Gloria went through the same kind of thing with her daughter—I mean, son. Sorry. She taught me some things about what you were probably going through. We know better now."

Frank looked tearful. "I'm sorry we didn't handle things well, honey. We were scared for you. We just wanted you to be safe, and we didn't know what we were doing."

Scenario Analysis

This was new territory for Erica and her parents. After no communication, the three of them were chatting more regularly and a face-to-face visit was likely to happen. Monica and Frank were eager to reconnect with their adult child. Over time they learned to invite information instead of snapping at things they didn't understand, asking questions and exploring what Erica had to say. It wasn't easy work, and they were still practicing. Listening with patience and kindness was reaping small rewards, though. As they acknowledged Erica's feelings, their calls with her began to feel like a relief. Rather than anxious dread, they all started looking forward to their Sunday afternoon video chats.

Parent Viewpoint

It had taken some time for Erica's parents to build up the courage to seek therapy. They felt ashamed of themselves for not knowing what to do and desperately missed their child after Erica had stopped communicating with them. Monica still didn't understand why anyone would want to change their gender. But she had come to decide that Erica's identity was nobody else's business, and to each their own. She thrilled at the possibility they might have their child back in their lives after the struggle they'd experienced. Frank felt a little sad at not having a son anymore, but he and the therapist agreed that was something for him to work on, and Erica didn't need to hear any such thing. He looked forward to getting to know the daughter he never knew he had.

Adult Child Viewpoint

Erica was tentatively hopeful after their last call. Her parents did seem thankful she had reached out and even eager to see her. Frank sounded like a dutiful student as he jumped to answer her question about ground rules, which showed he was taking everything seriously. She knew her parents were caring, decent people, but she was still hurting from the way they had condemned her. It was going to take time to gain back trust.

Strategy Breakdown

Even if you aren't dealing with gender identity or sexual orientation, the communication skills Frank and Monica used with Erica will be helpful to you.

If you have not been in touch with your child, and want to take the initiative to renew the relationship after a painful split, the path forward can be complicated. This situation is serious, and I suggest you seek professional counseling that fits your unique circumstances. If your child has expressly forbidden contact, honoring their wishes is probably best, at least for a time. If most of a year has passed, you could try to reach them with a birthday or other special occasion message via post or email. You need to respect boundaries, but you don't want them to think you have abandoned them. These choices are difficult ones to make.

If your overture gets a response, avoid being overly eager. For whatever reason, your child has found it necessary to set limits. If you can show you respect their time and attention, they will be more likely to want to approach you again.

It can be tempting to take drastic action to break the silence. But learning to sit with uncomfortable feelings without necessarily doing anything brings calm and peace to your family and may add other beneficial effects to your life: time for healing, opportunity for reflection, options for seeking advice. The bottom line is there's no need to pressure adults in your family to talk about anything if they say they don't want to. The skillful response when you meet resistance is to say something like *Thanks for letting me know. If things change, I'm here.* Subject closed. Then move on to something else.

If communication with your adult child is on hold, focus on improving your understanding of emotional states—your own and those of others. Time and again, clients have told me how this new focus led to unexpected improvements in their careers, friendships, and general quality of life. Our culture doesn't offer much in the way of instruction or examples, so you will have to seek information that appeals to you. It's a worthwhile, lifelong subject to study.

Potential Pitfalls

You have a lifetime to repair the ruptures or rifts with your children; usually, it's possible to reach some connection. Stay steady, exercise patience, and get support to avoid unfortunate behaviors like these:

Judging. As a rule, refrain from judging and criticizing your child—the type of work they do, their attire or weight, their personal habits, or their relationship choices. Other adults don't need your permission or approval for how they live their lives.

Prying. Unless you've established a rapport and trust about these matters, do not remark on or inquire about your child's relationship status or parenthood plans. These subjects may cause grief or hit a sore spot. People don't divulge everything, even to their parents. You don't know what losses—like breakups, miscarriages, or abortions—they may have been through.

Avoiding immature behavior. Do not comment unfavorably on their partner or their single status. Avoid contemptuous behavior like rolling your eyes sarcastically or making snippy comments.

Tips to Remember

» **Find common ground.** Families can survive having different religious or political viewpoints. Still, to maintain a sense of connection, they must share values of mutual respect and acceptance. Erica's parents demonstrated a commitment to making repairs in the relationship by reading and discussing trans lives with knowledgeable people and participating in their own therapy.

» **Start by listening.** If, like so many these days, your family has been affected by differences in personal values, think about what actions you would be willing to take to make things better. The willingness to listen or to ask your family member to educate you about their viewpoint is key. Again, this goal is only realistic if they, too, offer some reciprocity and are interested in sharing ideas.

Steps toward Reconnection

Everyone likes to discuss interests and things they are excited about. If a difficult conversation or a communication gap has occurred in your family, keep your attention on positive topics. Doing so does not mean you need to be fake or only talk about superficial things. You are attempting to rebuild a connection that became fragile or broken, so treading lightly is reasonable until you have regained some trust.

Find out what has been giving your adult child pleasure lately or making them laugh.

What groups or communities do they belong to these days?

Are there any events or plans they are looking forward to or hoping for?

Do they follow thinkers or leaders who provide them with strength or a feeling of purpose?

You can take your time; these questions are personal and best savored slowly, but they could result in fun or inspiring conversations that show your motivation to make things better between you and your estranged child.

The Visit

Alice and Keith were thrilled. In a few weeks, they would be hosting their daughter Marian, her husband, and their three grandkids who were flying cross-country to stay with them. It was the first time in several years they would all be together. "The kids are going to be so big we'll hardly recognize them by now! What games should we get for them?" wondered Alice. "I'll have to ask Marian what they like to do nowadays. Oh, it's been such a long time!" Keith was happy to clean up the lawn furniture and get the yard shipshape so the kids could play outside.

But a few days before the visit, Marian told her mother she booked a hotel for the visit. Alice was dismayed. "I didn't say much when she told me," Alice said to her husband, "but I thought a family visit meant they'd be staying with us."

Keith was disappointed to hear the news, and he knew Alice's feelings were hurt.

"I don't know why I feel so bad. I feel like I could cry." She sighed and looked distant. "They're going to be busy. It's not going to be as homey as I thought."

Alice knew Marian probably had a lot on her mind planning the trip on top of all her other responsibilities, but the misunderstanding nagged at her. She felt she should let her daughter know of her upset. She didn't want any tension when they arrived, and Marian would pick up Alice's mood being off. So she called her daughter.

"Is this a good time?" she asked when Marian picked up. "Kind of, Mom. Sure, I can talk a couple minutes. What's up?"

Scenario Analysis

Eventually, young families create their own traditions and some of those will inevitably disrupt the rituals you counted on earlier in life. Alice expected the visit to be the same as their previous one, not thinking about how Marian's family had grown and reconfigured. Young adults have complicated lives and sometimes sizable networks. Not only are they likely to have a spouse, but there may also be an ex-spouse and stepfamily relationships, perhaps including children as well as adults. Add two sets of in-laws to the mix, and they have a lot of connections to maintain. That new families create rhythms and routines to fit their lives is only natural. Meanwhile, the older generation may have retired or may just have fewer connections than before, with various losses reducing their social networks.

Parent Viewpoint

Alice missed Marian. They had always been close, but clearly Marian had her hands full at this time in her life, leaving little room for keeping in touch with Alice. They still had brief video chats or phone conversations, but not the confiding, thoughtful exchanges they used to. Alice had hoped for some of Marian's attention so her concerns about the visit could be heard, and yet it became apparent that was not possible.

She was disappointed, but felt compassion for Marian. "It's okay if you can't talk much," she said to her daughter. "I just wanted to let you know I misunderstood you about the visit. I thought you were staying at the house with us. It wasn't what I expected and I just wanted to air that out. Thank you for listening. I know it's going to be a great visit. I can't wait to see you." Alice was surprised at the relief she felt just from giving this quick explanation.

Adult Child Viewpoint

Marian was stretched thin by the early years of parenting. She didn't realize how complex the demands would feel—managing deadlines and obligations at her job, dealing with school and childcare schedules, all while trying to ensure her relationship with her husband would withstand the pressure. She was really looking forward to seeing her parents and could use some debriefing time with her mom. But how could her mother think everyone could fit in that small house without driving each other crazy?

"I'm sorry that got lost in the shuffle, Mom," Marian said. "But you don't have to worry, we'll definitely fit in time to connect! I already talked to Brian about planning a few outings with Dad and the kids, so you and I could have time to ourselves. The kids have friends coming over so I have to go. But thanks for checking in! We'll talk soon! Love you!"

Strategy Breakdown

Staying on good terms as a grandparent means exercising a lot of flexibility and acceptance. Living at a distance from family means plans are likely to change and visits could involve complicated arrangements. Regrettably, people are usually stressed and tired when traveling and not always at their best in terms of emotional control and self-awareness. Be prepared to use healthy communication strategies, not only when you're in touch from far away, but also when you're finally together again in person.

Here's how Alice managed her hurt feelings without triggering an argument with Marian:

Offer respect and honesty. Alice knew Marian had a lot going on and didn't want to burden her. She took the opportunity to speak candidly, one adult to another, avoiding conflict by staying conversational and not employing blame. Alice shared with Marian her own perceptions ("I misunderstood" and "I thought") and confusion ("It wasn't what I expected").

Express gratitude. Expressing thanks can be a powerful way to affirm your connection with someone. Once Alice had expressed even briefly what was bothering her, she felt a sense of ease, knowing Marian might understand her emotional state. She realized she didn't need Marian to change her plans or apologize. She just wanted to say how she felt and have Marian hear her. Thanking her daughter for that bridged the distance between the two of them. Knowing Marian listened to her was a way for Alice to feel close and connected to her daughter.

Keep communications short and sweet. Knowing Marian was too busy for a long conversation actually helped Alice express herself. When people know they have a time limit, they are more likely to choose their words carefully and get to the point. People can get distressed when they think discussing their feelings will be a drawn-out, exhausting experience. Sometimes I ask families to take two or three minutes to check in about an issue while I listen. They are often amazed at how much they can address in that short period. You won't reach an agreement or make any plan in two minutes, but stating your thoughts within that short period of time can be liberating.

Potential Pitfalls

Let's face it—that you, the parent, usually have to be the bigger person is not fair. Why is doing so worth making the effort? You get better results. And with repetition, you'll influence your children to become generous and kind people, like you. Watch for these potential problematic approaches:

Throwing a tantrum. It takes maturity to cope with changes in plans. Getting stuck and insisting things go as you initially expected will not make your children want to spend more time with you.

Refusing to adjust. Unless you have a disability that requires accommodation, try to be the one who accommodates your adult child as much as possible. Their life is probably more demanding and crowded with obligations than yours.

Using emotional blackmail. Parents want connection to their children, yet we cannot bring young people closer to the family through guilt or persuasion. Trying to manipulate family members to attend events or spend time with parents will not get us the love and affection we're looking for. Your adult child must give these things freely.

Tips to Remember

» **Stick to brief conversations.** Remember to appreciate the value of brevity in addressing emotions when working through a conflict. Like bite-size snacks of feeling, these short conversations can provide nourishing human connection.

» **Diminish your expectations.** Show understanding toward your adult child and avoid making demands on their time, especially after they become parents. They will see you as a welcome refuge they can count on rather than one more task they need to attend to.

» **Do all you can to enrich your own life.** Doing so will make you delighted to hear from your adult child, and you will have tales of your own to share when they do get in touch. They don't want to feel like you're sitting at home waiting for the phone to ring.

» **Keep up with technology and stay connected.** Arrange a regular schedule for phone or video calls with your adult child or with your grandchildren, depending on their ages. Older kids can take a few minutes on Sunday evening to talk with faraway relatives about sports, media, friends, or their pets. Since kids are so used to communicating online, it's entirely natural for them.

» **Accept what's possible.** Maybe your son-in-law wants his immediate family to spend Mother's Day with his folks this year. You can all enjoy a simple dinner midweek or the weekend after. When the young family has too many places to visit on Thanksgiving, suggest leftovers and fresh pie at your place the following week. If what you want is the pleasure of their company, your family can make up your own rules in whatever way works best for everyone.

Steps toward Reconnection

After a misunderstanding or disappointment with long-distance family, getting on the phone or online to reconnect is worth the effort. Start by checking whether you have the person's full attention or if they want to try for another time.

With a serious argument or significant troubles, you always have the option of writing a card instead of calling. Writing gives the other person time to think over their response and prevents the flare-ups and confusion that can come with text and other instant communication forms.

Keep contact going through various methods. Cards, small token gifts, online games, phone calls when convenient—all these small connections give a sense of moving through time together and remaining part of one another's lives.

Reflection Questions

» Because of situations such as immigration and work travel, many families must wrestle with managing long-distance relationships. How has distance shaped your family or your family history?

» Are there any justifiable reasons for family members to cut one another off? For how long? What message do you think they are trying to send by acting this way?

» How can parents handle unclear communication and provide guidance or helpful feedback to their children?

Conclusion: Parenting as a Practice

Congratulations! Whether you've read this book from cover to cover or concentrated on the chapters most relevant to your situation, you made a laudable investment in time and effort. I want to take this space to remind and reinforce what we've discussed through the course of this book. With continued practice, you will improve your communication skills, customizing the use of these strategies and tools to fit your own style and your family dynamics. Whatever obstacles you face, take courage and make the first move to reach out and reconnect with your adult child. You may not be perfect at what you've learned yet, but you now know enough to move forward with understanding and confidence.

Lessons Learned

I'd like to leave you with these essential final takeaways and encourage you to use, and refer to, this book repeatedly as your relationship with your adult child progresses and deepens. So here we'll review key lessons learned in this book for your convenient future reference. As these concepts become standard parts of your parenting practice, you'll build a communication foundation with your child that's natural, sincere, and is likely to get results.

Takeaway #1: Listen actively.

Want your life to change for the better? Practice this one principle. This set of skills will develop your concentration and empathic abilities so you can pick up the hidden meaning between the lines in a conversation. Review the details in chapter 2 (see page 13) whenever you need a reminder. Your reward will be stronger, closer relationships.

Takeaway #2: Validate and encourage.

Show you care by participating in a positive conversation. Offer compassion and understanding so your child knows you're on their team. Overdoing this part is impossible to do; talking in an encouraging, affirmative way has a magnetic effect on people. Your adult child will seek your counsel and trust you with their secrets when you affirm their talents, strengths, and value. A person inclined to give generous encouragement and say affirming things to other people provides a mood-booster to everyone around them.

Takeaway #3: Eliminate blame.

Everyone needs to be accountable for themselves, but blame has never done anybody any good in the realm of family relationships. Assigning fault like a traffic cop giving out tickets only makes people feel bad without providing any motivation to change their actions. If anything, blame is more likely to produce shame, isolation, and worse behavior. Addressing the issue is much more effective than trying to make people feel guilty.

Takeaway #4: Reduce defensive reactions.

Everybody occasionally displays defensiveness, a close cousin to blame. While this reaction is perfectly natural, letting defensiveness take over is not effective. When one person feels criticized by another or believes they have done poorly at something, they tend to go into attack mode to protect themselves. When we notice ourselves lapsing into defensive language, or feel physical sensations that cue us (like our heart speeding up or our face feeling hot), it's our job to grab the reins of our mood and get back in control. Often the best strategy is takeaway #5.

Takeaway #5: When in doubt, stop talking.

You'll be amazed how readily you can defuse conflict if you're willing to practice this challenging strategy. (Warning: Super-human effort may be involved.) In heated moments, we usually want nothing more than to get our point across. Knowing when you're making matters worse, though, is essential. And that doesn't mean you should just clam up and refuse to participate. Practice graciously pausing a discussion: "I don't think we're getting anywhere. Let's take a break and try again later."

Takeaway #6: Setting boundaries = self-care.

Setting limits and boundaries means giving other people a fair warning of how far you can go before you run out of gas. Don't let your tank run dry and then start yelling at them, because they didn't know you were getting drained. Mothers are especially prone to acting this way. Our culture trains moms to do so much selfless caring for others, that by the time they notice they're out of energy or supplies, there's nothing left to do but get mad at everybody around them. If you're feeling guilty about putting up boundaries or taking time to recharge, read about these practices in chapter 2 (see page 13).

First Steps Toward Your Goals

We're at an excellent place to return to the goals you set for yourself and your relationship with your adult child back in chapter 1 (see page 7). Have these goals changed at all as events have occurred or as you read this book? If they have, what are your new goals for reconnection?

Reaching any goal begins with the first step. Below are some options for getting off to a good start in some common scenarios. Reading them will likely spark other ideas for your situation.

If your goal is related to strengthening ties with your child:

Set a new communication habit. Regularity will help, so suggest a weekly phone call or, time and distance permitting, a date to accompany each other on a necessary activity. Make a grocery trip together, pull weeds, or paint each other's nails.

If you're establishing new boundaries with an adult child living at home again:

Consider what you need. What routines, habits, or spaces are important to preserve your well-being? Do you need quiet at a regular hour? The dining room table kept clear so you can do sewing projects? Think it out yourself, then invite your child to collaborate on the ground rules and share their own needs, so you are both clear with one another. Plan to meet regularly to assess how things are going.

If your adult child hasn't moved out:

Start small. Starting with small changes is only fair, whether you're encouraging them to find their own housing, or you just want a different dynamic under your roof. Give plenty of advance notice. Avoid adding to their financial pressures if that is a factor. If you want them to participate or contribute more to the household, start by asking what they can offer instead of making demands.

If living with them is tense:

Remember that parenting an adult is different. The parent should treat the adult child living with them as an adult in terms of boundaries and respectfulness. Hold conversations in common areas instead of standing in the doorway of their room. Propose meeting and discussion times with one to two days' advance notice. Show you are friendly and warm but also have household business to take care of. Acting as if you're still parenting a child will bring out the worst in both of you.

If you're out of touch with them:

Tread lightly. Adult children who are distant, uncommunicative, or back in touch after a prolonged cutoff require a delicate approach to avoid setbacks and to rebuild the relationship. If the reconnection is difficult, seek counseling from a specialized professional who has experience with these situations or a trusted family member who has rapport and may act as an intermediary.

Play the Long Game

Whether you haven't been communicating at all or you'd just like to be closer, reconnecting with your adult children will be an ongoing process rather than a one-time event. When there are setbacks or disappointments, don't give up on the connection goals you set in chapter 1 (see page 7). Whatever efforts you are willing to make are likely to prove worthwhile in the long run. You can always return to this book to refresh your skills.

Look back and appreciate how long raising your child took. Then look to all the years ahead when you'll have the privilege and pleasure of maintaining a close relationship with this younger adult. If we get stuck wishing we had the earlier years of our parenthood to live over again, the possibilities that await us can get eclipsed. The rich experience of cherishing someone over decades is much more expansive than raising children to graduate from high school. You may still have the best years ahead of you as a family.

Success Story

I'd like to end on a positive note with an update on Ben from chapter 4 and his parents, April and Pete. You'll recall that Ben was the carefree carpenter who would periodically drop by and "borrow" money from his parents. April got his attention by setting limits and telling him she wasn't okay with him asking for cash anymore.

Like his son, Pete preferred to avoid conflict but he came through for April and backed her up on this issue. Pete told Ben that since Ben was single and had no children, he was the son they would have to rely on for support. Pete asked Ben to plan two weekends a month to do repairs on their house and help him with chores in exchange for the money Pete would have paid someone else for this work. Ben declined to take payment for his work "since it's for the family," and followed through as requested. His brothers were so impressed, they thanked him for helping out when they were unable to due to their family obligations.

Soon Ben, who had been the baby of the family, was making everyone proud. He was getting positive attention for contributing instead of being mocked for being a slacker.

These affirmations began to affect Ben's self-image. He still liked to kid around and have fun, but he felt gratified that people appreciated him shouldering more work than required. Feeling capable and getting praise for his skills and careful work gave him a sense of pride and accomplishment. His bluster and bragging was replaced with genuine confidence, and he became a more generous and sincere person overall. He wasn't just a screw-off anymore who did as little as possible. At work, showing an interest and taking his job seriously gained him the respect of newer apprentices and other journeymen carpenters.

Looking Ahead

We often want so much for our children that we hold high standards for our parental responsibilities. It can be challenging to look at our parenting, but you're up to the task. I encourage you to reject perfection and consider "good enough" parenting as a goal, and to model that for your child if they're raising kids of their own. You may be mending generations of hurt or grief through your learning. Any changes you make, imperfect as they may be, could lay the foundation for a better future. All good wishes to you in reconnecting with your adult child!

Resources

Arnett, Jeffrey, and Elizabeth Fishel. *Getting to 30: A Parent's Guide to the 20-Something Years.* New York: Workman Publishing, 2014.

Up-to-date research on the new field of emerging adulthood, a social phenomenon related to economic and societal changes prolonging the transition from adolescent to adult.

Coleman, Joshua. *When Parents Hurt: Compassionate Strategies for When You and Your Grown Child Don't Get Along.* New York: William Morrow and Company, 2008.

Includes a cultural and historic perspective on family relationships; addresses guilt, mismatches, and other factors contributing to the suffering parents experience. An excellent, informative read.

Gilbertson, Tina. *Reconnecting with Your Estranged Adult Child.* Novato, CA: New World Library, 2020.

If your child has cut you out of their life, this book is what you need. Well-informed, specific guidance for parents who are hurt and confused; written with wit and sensitivity.

Isay, Jane. *Walking on Eggshells: Navigating the Delicate Relationship Between Adult Children and Parents.* New York: Broadway Books, 2008.

Written with sensitivity and wisdom, this book is based on probing and thoughtful interviews by an author of several books on trends and themes in family relationships.

Konstam, Varda. *Parenting Your Emerging Adult: Launching Kids from 18 to 29.* Far Hills, NJ: New Horizon Press, 2013.

Clear guidance for parents whose child has moved back in with them; includes stories and anecdotes of real families, including the author's.

Waltz, Samantha, ed. *Blended: Writers on the Stepfamily Experience*. Berkeley, CA: Seal Press, 2015.

The inside view of stepfamilies, this anthology includes humor, losses, confessionals, and an honest look at the complexity involved in merging bank accounts, siblings, and kitchenware.

References

Al-Anon Family Groups. Accessed March 22, 2021. Al-Anon.org.

Arnett, Jeffrey Jensen. "Emerging Adulthood: A Theory of Development from the Late Teens through the Twenties." *American Psychologist* 55, no. 5 (2000): 469–480. doi: 10.1037//0003-066X.55.5.469.

Brockmeier, Erica K. "To Err Is Human, to Learn, Divine." *Penn Today* (May 2020). PennToday.upenn.edu/news /err-human-learn-divine.

Davis, Shirley. "The Neuroscience of Shame." CPTSD Foundation. April 2019. CPTSDFoundation.org/2019/04/11 /the-neuroscience-of-shame.

Ducharme, Jamie. "More Millennials Are Dying 'Deaths of Despair,' as Overdose and Suicide Rates Climb." *Time* (June 13, 2019). Time.com/5606411/millennials-deaths -of-despair.

Fry, Richard, Jeffrey S. Passel, and D'Vera Cohen. "A Majority of Young Adults in the U.S. Live with Their Parents for the First Time Since the Great Depression." Pew Research Center. September 2020. PewResearch.org/fact-tank/2020/09/04

/a-majority-of-young-adults-in-the-u-s-live-with-their
-parents-for-the-first-time-since-the-great-depression.

Kerr, Emma. "See 10 Years of Average Total Student Loan
Debt." *U.S. News and World Report* (September 15, 2020).
USNews.com/education/best-colleges/paying-for-college
/articles/see-how-student-loan-borrowing-has-risen-in
-10-years.

Lebowitz, Eli R. "'Failure to Launch': Shaping Intervention for
Highly Dependent Adult Children." *Journal of the American
Academy of Child and Adolescent Psychiatry* 55, no. 2
(2016): 89–90. doi: 10.1016/j.jaac.2015.10.014.

Lisitsa, Ellie. "Parenting as Your Kids Grow Up." The Gottman
Institute. June 6, 2012. Gottman.com/blog/parenting-as
-your-kids-grows-up.

Maldonado, Camilo. "Price of College Increasing Almost
8 Times Faster Than Wages." *Forbes* (July 2018).
Forbes.com/sites/camilomaldonado/2018/07/24/price-of
-college-increasing-almost-8-times-faster-than-wages
/?sh=6116678e66c1.

Mazzara, Alicia. "Census: Income-Rent Gap Grew in 2018."
Center on Budget and Policy Priorities. September 27,
2019. CBPP.org/blog/census-income-rent-gap
-grew-in-2018.

Stillman, Jessica. "Use the Magic 5:1 Ratio to Improve All Your
Relationships." *Inc.* (July 2020). Inc.com/jessica-stillman
/use-magic-51-ratio-to-improve-all-your-relationships.html.

Taylor, Paul, and Rich Morin. "Forty Years After Woodstock, a
Gentler Generation Gap." Pew Research Center. August
12, 2009. PewResearch.org/social-trends/2009/08/12
/forty-years-after-woodstockbra-gentler-generation-gap/.

Index

Acknowledgments

I would like to thank some of the writers who have influenced my understanding of belonging and family:

Madeleine L'Engle	Astrid Lindgren	Anne Patchett
Shirley Jackson	Zora Neale Hurston	Barbara Kingsolver
Mary Shelley	Sarah Waters	Deborah Tannen
Silvia Federici	Amy Tan	Nell Dunn
Kate Bornstein	Donna Tartt	Gerald Durrell

About the Author

Kate McNulty, LCSW, is a long-time resident of Portland, Oregon. She has two adult children and appreciates them for keeping her abreast of popular culture and contemporary thought. When Kate is not writing or seeing therapy clients, she hikes, enjoys making music, and does arts and crafts. She is the author of *Love and Asperger's*. Visit her at Portland-Counseling.com or AutisticTherapist.com.

CPSIA information can be obtained
at www.ICGtesting.com
Printed in the USA
JSHW042100170721
16980JS00001B/1

9 781648 769436